FUN DAY TRIPS
FOR ALL AGES

EASY CYCLING

around VANCOUVER

Expanded and Updated

JEAN & NORMAN
• • • **COUSINS**

GREYSTONE BOOKS

D&M PUBLISHERS INC.

Vancouver/Toronto/Berkeley

Greystone Books
An imprint of D&M Publishers Inc.
2323 Quebec Street, Suite 201
Vancouver BC Canada V5T 4S7
www.greystonebooks.com

Cataloguing data available from Library and Archives Canada
ISBN 978-1-55365-582-4 (pbk.)
ISBN 978-1-55365-829-0 (ebook)

Editing by Lucy Kenward
Copyediting by Maja Grip and Lara Kordic
Cover design by Jessica Sullivan
Text design by Naomi MacDougall
Cover photograph by Toby Adamson/Axiom Photographic Agency/Getty Images
Photos by Norman Cousins
Maps by Eric Leinberger
Printed and bound in Canada by Friesens
Text printed on acid-free, 100% post-consumer paper
Distributed in the U.S. by Publishers Group West

We gratefully acknowledge the financial support of the Canada Council for the Arts, the British Columbia Arts Council, the Province of British Columbia through the Book Publishing Tax Credit and the Government of Canada through the Canada Book Fund for our publishing activities.

Every attempt has been made to ensure that the information in this book is accurate and up to date; however, the authors and publisher assume no liability for any loss, damage, inconvenience or injury that may occur to anyone using this book. All outdoor activities involve an element of the unknown and thus an element of risk, and you are solely responsible for your own safety and health at all times. Always check local conditions, know your own limitations and consult a map.

CONTENTS

. . . . .

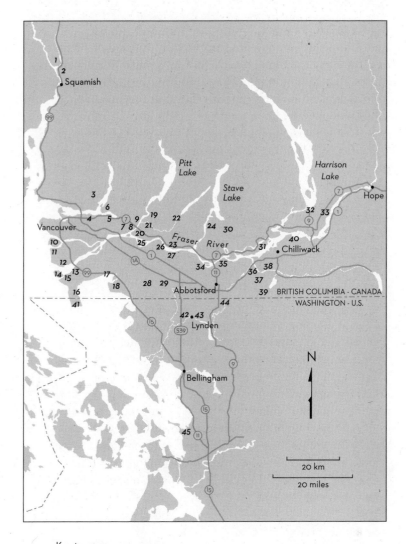

Pitt
Lake

Stave
Lake

Harrison
Lake

1

2
• Squamish

99

3

6

4 *5*

Vancouver

9 *19* *22*
7 *8* *21*
20
25 *26* *23*
27

24 *30*

Fraser River

7

31

32 *33*
9

40
• Chilliwack

7
• Hope

1

10
11

12

13

14 *15*

99

17

18

1A

34 *35*

36 *38*
37

28 *29*

Abbotsford

39

BRITISH COLUMBIA · CANADA
WASHINGTON · U.S.

16

41

15

42 • *43*
• Lynden

539

• Bellingham

44

9

N

• Bellingham

15

45

11

20 km

20 miles

> INTRODUCTION

In revising and updating this book we have explored new roads and trails and combined them to form new routes that fit our criteria for *Easy Cycling around Vancouver*. We have re-routed existing rides that have been altered by development or changes in road usage—everywhere becomes busier—and we have taken out some rides that are no longer satisfactory. We have added some more off-road cycling by making use of the expanding network of greenways and trails around Vancouver. We have also introduced one or two urban routes.

Like the previous edition, this book is designed to encourage beginning cyclists, families and older or perhaps "rusty" cyclists to get out on their bikes and explore at whatever level is appropriate for them. Our cycling philosophy remains the same: We cycle for pleasure and discovery. We do not aim to reach our destination in the shortest possible time; we stop when the fancy takes us. We don't regard cycling as a sport or a challenge—although effort does go into it. Cycling is fun, inexpensive and kind to the environment. Best of all, it lifts the spirits to travel at the leisurely pace unique to this activity, exploring the byways on a personal journey of discovery.

The routes in *Easy Cycling* are just an example of the many options available. Perhaps some of you, after gaining experience and confidence from these rides, will be encouraged to join a local cycling club. Community centres, outdoor clubs and some bicycle shops organize group rides similar to those described in this book. The Vancouver Area Cycling Coalition organizes a series of Great Rides and other bike events throughout the year. Through organizations such as these, you will be introduced to the cycling possibilities around the city.

Do not be afraid to put together your own cycle tour, perhaps based on one or two of our rides in the Fraser Valley or Washington. Arm yourself with a detailed map (International Travel Maps & Books, 12300 Bridgeport Road in Richmond is a good source) and pick out some secondary roads to link up with the routes in *Easy Cycling*. Arrange convenient overnight accommodation along the way, pack your panniers and set off. You will have embarked on a freewheeling style of holiday that knows no boundaries.

The forty-five rides presented are short—between 10 and 45 kilometres. They are routed on paved roads, on good gravel surfaces and occasionally on informal trails. Most use safe, rural roads and avoid areas of heavy traffic as much as possible. Many are circular tours. You will notice that many of the rides are located in the Fraser Valley and northwestern Washington. We've tried to cover most areas around Vancouver in our collection, including Squamish to the north and Harrison to the east, but some parts of the Lower Mainland, though delightful, do not lend themselves to easy cycling. Similarly, we omit popular city cycle routes and paths (which are well covered in other books) because they fall outside our category of countrified tours.

A descriptive summary precedes each ride, enabling you to find a route that's appropriate for your riding ability. A following paragraph gives an overview of the area or mentions places and facts of local interest. Sometimes optional routes or side trips are suggested. In most cases, the recommended lunch stop offers a picnic table or bench, often in a park. The Bicycles and Equipment section offers practical advice on bicycles, equipment and clothing, with hints on comfort for the beginning and out-of-practice cyclist. An important section on safety will help to reassure the fearful and encourage responsible cycling.

Researching and revising these rides has been a pleasure—there have been new neighbourhoods and byways to explore and beautiful parks and picnic spots to discover. What you make of the rides is up to you. The French have a delightful expression for being out and about on a bicycle: They describe it as being *en vélo*. We hope that you will enjoy being *en vélo* around Vancouver.

> HOW TO USE THIS BOOK

We hope you will start by reading and becoming familiar with the following introductory chapters. If you're an experienced cyclist, the advice may be unnecessary; but if you're a novice, you will benefit from the recommendations, at least in the beginning.

Until you have some experience cycling, it is a good idea to start with short and easy rides, building your confidence and ability until you can judge what you are capable of.

How do you choose a short, easy ride? At the beginning of every ride description is a list of features:

ROUND-TRIP DISTANCE: The rides in this book range from 10 to 45 kilometres.

TERRAIN: Our routes mainly follow paved roads, but this section tells you if you will also encounter gravel dykes or shared footpaths and whether the ride is level or hilly.

TRAFFIC VOLUME: We try to avoid busy roads, but it isn't always possible. Here we tell you how much car traffic to expect.

TIME TO ALLOW: This section suggests the approximate length of time you will need for the round trip. Our estimate includes a lunch break of 30 minutes plus up to 30 minutes extra if there are unpaved roads, hills or other features that might slow you down. The range indicated—e.g., 2 ½ to 3 ½ hours—allows for riders' different paces.

HIGHLIGHTS: We point out scenery and items of interest you may enjoy. This still leaves plenty for you to discover for yourself.

PICNIC SPOT: Whenever we can suggest a suitable spot for a picnic, we do. Most sites fall about two-thirds of the way through the ride's total distance.

STARTING POINT AND HOW TO GET THERE: This section gives you instructions on where to start the ride and how to get to that spot by road or by transit. We usually transport our bikes by car to the starting point. We give road instructions to reach the starting point of each ride, and we've done our best to find suitable places to leave a car, most often in municipal or regional parks that are easy to locate. There are increasingly more options to get around.

If you plan to ride near the area where you live, you might be able to reach the starting point by using a neighbourhood cycle route, such as the Frances-Union Bikeway in Burnaby or the Railway and Garden City Bikeways in Richmond. The City of Vancouver has 300 kilometres of on- and off-road bikeways, such as the Central Valley Greenway linking Vancouver, Burnaby and New Westminster, and the Midtown and Ridgeway Bikeways running east to west across the city. Several bridges across the Fraser River now have dedicated bicycle lanes, including the bridge beside the Canada Line SkyTrain route linking Marine Drive Station to Bridgeport Station. In each municipality, bicycle maps and descriptions of local trails can be obtained from city hall and often from community centres, or downloaded from their websites.

Transit might be an option for some. All Metro buses carry a limited number of bicycles, as do SkyTrain, SeaBus and the West Coast Express; a free shuttle service transports cyclists through the George Massey Tunnel. Greyhound services Squamish and Bellingham (bicycles must be boxed), and Amtrak will transport riders and their bikes with a reservation; northern Washington State also has buses equipped with bike racks. We encourage you to check schedules and be flexible with your plans: The West Coast Express commuter train, for example, runs weekdays only and in set directions at specific times of day; SkyTrain has some restrictions on carrying bikes during rush hour, and the shuttle through the George Massey Tunnel runs at one- or two-hour intervals and on a reduced schedule from October to May. Information on these options and more can be found in the latest edition of TransLink's *Metro Vancouver Cycling Map*, available wherever maps are sold, and on the TransLink website. The website also features handy trip planners to help you work out your approach by transit or by bike (or a combination of both).

WHEN TO GO: Here we note any seasonal attractions and events.

CONNECTS WITH: Rides that are adjacent to or slightly overlap with others are noted here, allowing you to combine the routes for a longer ride.

Now that you know how to discover what is in a ride, you can begin to make choices.

Our route instructions use the elapsed distance from the starting point to help identify turnings or alert you to points of interest. You can keep track of these distances with a bicycle computer if you have one; otherwise simply use the figures as a guide together with landmarks and other information in the route descriptions. Because of a number of factors such as surface conditions and the computer's calibration, these figures may not always be accurate. Do not be dismayed if you come across minor discrepancies between the distance you have travelled and what we have written down.

Our maps are intended as a guide to be used in conjunction with the route instructions. We strongly recommend that you carry a standard map of the area, such as MapArt's *Greater Vancouver & Fraser Valley* mapbook or TransLink's *Metro Vancouver Cycling Map*, at all times. If you get off course, you'll find the complete picture helpful for getting you back on track.

You might find it convenient to photocopy the route instructions and the map for easy reference on the ride. You can keep these handy in a pocket or in the map case on the top of a cycling handlebar bag. The rides are laid out on facing pages in the book, so they are easy to copy.

If you can, start early in the day before the roads become too busy. Note that on summer weekends the parks also can be very crowded.

You're ready to set out on your chosen ride. One thing will lead to another, and before long you'll discover for yourself other byroads to explore on your bicycle.

Touring and Hybrid Bicycles

If you already own a bicycle, you'll probably want to use it for these rides, and who are we to say you shouldn't? However, some types of bike are more suitable for our purpose than others.

We prefer a "hybrid" bike, though you could also use a touring bike. Both of these are intermediate bikes (between the extremes of racing and mountain bikes) appropriate for our intermediate rides. They combine wider, more stable tires and a more comfortable seat and upright riding position than racing bikes, and they are faster and lighter than mountain bikes.

Racing bikes and mountain bikes were designed for purposes other than the leisurely meanderings we describe. But if you already own one of these types of bike, you can use it on these rides. Cycling these routes is enjoyable, no matter what your choice of bike.

About Bicycle Fitting

Many cyclists, including long-time owners, have not adjusted their bikes for proper efficiency. While this is not crucial for local shopping trips, it will make a difference in comfort and safety on longer rides. The subject of bicycle fitting is too detailed to cover properly in this book, so in addition to the tips below ask for on-the-spot advice at a bicycle shop or refer to a book on bicycle maintenance.

Bicycles are manufactured in various frame sizes for people of different stature. Once you've chosen a frame size, you can adjust the bike at several points to make it comfortable for you. For instance:

> Saddle posts can be moved up or down.

> Saddles can be moved backward or forward, and their front end tilted up or down.

> Handlebars can be raised or lowered.

Your bike adjustments are correct if:

> When you sit on the bike, your leg is almost, but not quite, straight at the lowest point of your pedal revolution. If it is not, you are losing some of the downward force your legs are capable of producing. Your knees are lined up over your feet so you are not straining your hips, knees or ankles.

> Your handlebars are within easy reach, and your body is not angled too far forward. Your back is flat rather than rounded, and your neck, shoulders and wrists are relaxed.

> You are not slipping forward or backward on your saddle.

Correct leg position at bottom of stroke

Getting these adjustments right is essential. If they are not correct, you will tire easily and be uncomfortable to the point where you will not enjoy cycling and might give it up. So it's worth taking the trouble to ensure that you are completely at ease on your bike.

Bicycle Essentials and Accessories

Most touring and hybrid bikes come well equipped for touring, but those that don't can easily be fitted with the desired equipment. Some bikes come with shocks (suspension), but they are not really necessary for these rides. Ideally, your bike should have:

MEDIUM TIRES. A tire between 1 ⅜ inches and 1 ¾ inches wide is suited to both paved roads and reasonably smooth gravel dykes. A slightly raised tread helps the tire grip on uneven surfaces.

STRONG BRAKES. Cantilever and V-brakes are widely used, and both have strong pulling power.

EIGHTEEN SPEEDS OR MORE. A range of gears is good because it includes easier gears for hill climbing.

Warning of approaching danger   Toeclip

A REAR-VIEW MIRROR. This is one of the most important safety accessories you can have. A medium to large mirror attached to the handlebars lets you see more than a tiny one attached to a helmet.

MUDGUARDS. When you're caught in a rainstorm, these tire protectors (sometimes called fenders) will prevent you from getting soaked in the spray from your tires.

A REAR LUGGAGE RACK AND PANNIER(S). The metal rack bolts to your bike so you can carry panniers. These saddle bags can hold your rain gear, lunch, extra clothing, tools, farm produce, etc. A bungee strap on top of your rack is a convenient way to hold articles of clothing you may want to slip on or off. While we much prefer panniers, which keep the bikes balanced and our backs free of sweat, others use a well-padded and lightweight backpack to carry their gear.

A HANDLEBAR BAG. This bag can carry items to which you want easy access, such as emergency tools, rags, energy rations, sunscreen, cash, a camera, maps and route instructions.

TOECLIPS. These curved plastic or metal pieces fasten onto the front of your pedals to properly position your feet. Adjustable straps hold your feet in place. Toeclips force you to put your weight onto the ball of your foot, which is the most efficient position for getting the most power from your pedal stroke. If you are a novice rider, delay fitting toeclips to your pedals until you feel totally comfortable on

Equipped for easy cycling

your bike. Always make sure the fasteners are loose enough to allow you to withdraw your shoes quickly when necessary, and remember to pull your feet backward before dismounting.

A WARNING DEVICE, MOST COMMONLY A BELL. A bell is required by law, and it is particularly useful to warn others on a shared pathway that you are approaching. Please do not ride at high speed, ring your bell, then expect other users to avoid *you*.

A WATER BOTTLE AND CARRIER. The metal or plastic cage fits on your bike frame and holds a water bottle. Drink often; dehydration can be a serious risk when you're exerting yourself.

A BICYCLE PUMP AND A PRESSURE GAUGE. If the pump doesn't come with a mount, you may need to fasten it to the bike's frame with accessory clips that you can obtain at a bicycle shop. Make sure the pump fits the valve on the inner tube in your tire and keep your tires properly inflated. (The maximum pressure is noted on the side of the tire itself.)

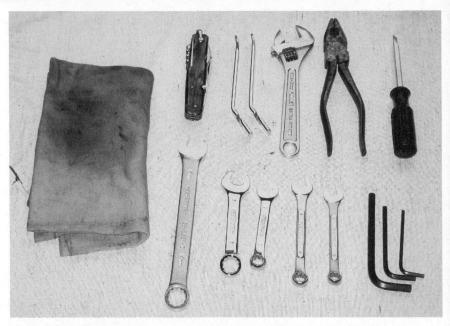

Left: rag for wiping oily hands; Top, left to right: penknife, tire levers, adjustable wrench, pliers, two-ended screwdriver; Bottom, left to right: 15mm, 13mm, 10mm, 9mm and 8mm wrenches, CR-V6, CR-V4 and CR-V3 Allen keys

A SPARE INNER TUBE, TIRE LEVERS AND A PATCH KIT. Tire punctures are the most common breakdown on a ride. Before you leave home, know how to change the tube; repairing the punctured one later is easier than trying to mend it on the spot. The spare should be the same size as the original tube. It may come with either a Schraeder (fat) valve or a Presta (thin) valve—it doesn't matter which, but the valve should be the same type as on the original tire.

A TOOL KIT. Bicycles are subject to constant vibration, causing components to loosen. Regular maintenance will prevent most problems, but there will be times when, for want of a simple adjustment, your bike becomes unrideable. You will need some basic tools in order to make these adjustments when out on a ride. BCAA members now get free roadside bicycle assistance with their membership, so in a real pinch you can call a mechanic to help you out.

In order that their edges don't become burred and eventually useless, your tools need to be an exact fit for the parts they're being used on. It is also essential to tighten parts firmly to prevent components from slipping. To be sure we get the right fit, we've found it useful to detach a nut from the bike, take it to a hardware store and select a wrench that exactly matches that part, be it either metric or SAE.

Nowadays, Allen keys (also known as hex keys) have largely replaced screwdrivers. Here again, it is essential that they fit exactly so as not to ruin the screw heads. Allen keys are not often available singly, so you may have to buy a full set of ten to fifteen keys—just carry with you the two or three that fit your bike.

We show here the tool kit we have assembled for our joint use. Your tools may very well be different sizes.

A FIRST-AID KIT. Unless you have special needs, a basic kit from the drugstore should see you through most situations.

AN ANTI-THEFT LOCK. We recommend a U-lock for maximum strength, or keep your bike within sight at all times.

LIGHTS. The rides described in this book are intended to be done in daylight, but the law requires you to use a white front light and a red rear light if you are out past dark.

If you are driving to the starting point, you will need a bicycle carrier. A variety of racks is available from bicycle and automotive retailers. (Note: If your bike rack is easily removable, lock it in the vehicle while you are out riding.)

Maintaining Your Bike

The following simple tasks will ensure that your bicycle is safe and enjoyable to ride:

> Check your tire pressure and add some air, especially if you haven't ridden for a while.

> Test the bolts holding your rack, mudguards (fenders), handlebar bag and bottle cage (water bottle carrier) every once in a while—especially after riding over rough surfaces— to make sure they're tight.

> Clean and lubricate the chain.

> Adjust your brakes and periodically replace brake pads and cables.

> Properly position gear-change guides to prevent the chain from slipping off the outside cogs.

Don't be put off by these maintenance duties. They don't need to be performed all that often, and if you aren't interested in doing them yourself bicycle maintenance shops will handle them for you. But they must be done by somebody; otherwise your bicycle will become unfit to ride.

Better yet, get a book or take a course on bicycle maintenance and become interested in what makes your bicycle work best.

A Suggested Wardrobe

Contrary to popular belief, you don't need to kit yourself out with expensive, specialized clothes—not, at any rate, for the type of cycling described in this book. Nevertheless, if that is what you fancy, bicycle shops carry a range of clothing (and other accessories) specially designed for cycling efficiency and stylishness.

Assuming that you'll undertake these rides from approximately April to October, you'll need to be prepared for weather ranging from cool to hot. The following should cover most eventualities:

HEADGEAR. Here you have no choice: The law in British Columbia requires you to wear a helmet. If you're not already a cyclist, you will have to buy a helmet certified by the Canadian Standards Association. Buy one at a bicycle shop and ask the staff to advise you on proper fit. A poorly adjusted or improperly secured helmet is itself a source of danger.

LAYERS FOR THE UPPER BODY. Try a T-shirt, a long-sleeved shirt, a sweater and a windproof and waterproof jacket (see rainwear). Outer layers can be pulled off as the day warms up. Bright colours will help passing traffic see you more easily. Some cyclists find quick-drying nylon or polyester more comfortable than cotton. When you progress to longer hours of cycling than these individual rides call for, you might want to try clothing made of lightweight silk, merino wool or synthetic layers to help keep you dry and warm and prevent chafing.

SHORTS. These are our preferred legwear; we simply find them less restrictive than long pants. If you choose to wear three-quarter-length capri-style pants, be sure the fabric doesn't catch in the chain and cause you to have an accident. To protect against saddle-soreness, you may want to buy specially padded cycling shorts or underwear that reduce the pressure on your seat. You can also buy a padded saddle cover.

SNEAKERS OR ATHLETIC SHOES. We find these types of shoes quite satisfactory provided they are not bulky, especially if you are using toeclips. Cleated cycling shoes are not necessary for our kind of cycling trips, which may include walking about in parks or buildings, but if you already own shoes with recessed cleats you will no doubt find them adequate for walking.

RAINWEAR. You can't go out cycling without being caught in a shower occasionally, and we suggest you carry simple, lightweight rainwear for these times. For comfort and safety, keep your torso dry with a waterproof jacket rather than a cape, which can billow in the wind and upset your balance. You can also wear waterproof pants, but we find them uncomfortable against bare legs and prefer to go without.

> CYCLING SAFETY

Cycling is not an inherently dangerous pastime. Popular opinion would like us to believe that we risk our lives when we venture onto the roads. Not so. The statistics suggest that cycling fatalities are among the lowest of many categories of recreational and non-recreational activity.

Nonetheless, cycling safety requires more than donning a helmet, which, as manufacturers warn, provides no protection to parts of the body that it does not cover. All cyclists can substantially reduce the possibility of accidents by following a few tried and true guidelines for minimizing cycling risk:

> Keep well to the right of the road, out of the way of overtaking traffic.

> Cycle in single file when travelling with others. Cycling abreast increases the risk to the outside rider and makes it more difficult for a driver to pass safely. Yes, we know that cycling in single file inhibits conversation, but it reduces risk.

> Leave 3 to 4 metres between you and the cyclist ahead of you, and don't allow another rider to follow closely behind you. A sudden stop or a change of direction by either one of you can cause a collision, knocking both of you off your bikes.

> Check your rear-view mirror frequently. Advance notice of traffic approaching from behind—including hell-bent cyclists—reduces surprises and consequently saves you from accidents.

> When riding downhill, raise your body slightly off the saddle to shift more weight onto the pedals. This body position, combined with the suppleness of your knees, gives you much better control over your bicycle if you hit a bump or other irregularity at speed. Resist the temptation to let loose on the downward grade; keep your speed to the point where you know you can brake to a full stop within the distance you can see. If you go too fast into a blind bend, you might swing wide over to the far side of the road and into oncoming traffic.

Right

Wrong

> Approach left turns with great care. Make your intentions clear by signalling with your arm. Move toward the middle of the road and make your turn when it is safe to do so. Don't ride across the path of oncoming traffic. If traffic is heavy, be prepared to dismount and walk your bicycle across two sides of the intersection. In short, you can't be too careful when turning left at busy intersections.

> Dismount and walk your bike across oblique railway tracks. If you want to ride across them, ensure that there's no road or rail traffic approaching the crossing from any direction. If there is, stop until it has passed. From a short distance back, ride to a position where you are facing the tracks at a ninety-degree angle. Cross the tracks straight on and resume your ride on the right side of the road.

> Wear eye shields, preferably slightly tinted wide-angle shields that will not impede your field of vision. If you cycle often, something— dust, insects, small pebbles—will fly into your eyes occasionally, possibly resulting in a fall. Light plastic shields will protect your eyes and usually prevent this kind of accident.

> Practise dismounting rapidly so that you can do this instinctively and safely if you must stop in a hurry.

> Keep an eye out for dogs, and stay calm when they appear without warning. Try not to brake suddenly or swerve. Often, the stern command "Stay!" will deter a chasing dog. In our experience, it is best to keep going; when you leave its territory, the dog will usually give up.

> Be watchful when passing parked cars. A door could be opened into your path.

> Obey the rules of the road, including stop signs and red lights. Cyclists have the same responsibilities and rights as drivers. The Motor Vehicle Act and municipal bylaws apply to cyclists, too. Do not ride on sidewalks except where it is specifically allowed. Even then, give pedestrians the right-of-way and pass them only at low speed. Walk your bike when using a pedestrian crossing.

> On dykes and trails, expect to meet walkers, dogs (which should be on a leash but often aren't), children, horses (which can be nervous)

and other cyclists. Ring your bell when approaching from behind and overtake slowly, not aggressively. Remember that most of these users have the right-of-way over cyclists.

Your safety is not a matter of chance; it is overwhelmingly in your own hands. Recognize the risks and what you can do to reduce them. Then, irksome though you may find them at first, follow these rules. By doing so, you reduce the risks of cycling because you put yourself in control.

In conclusion, we repeat that the first rule of cycling safety is to ride well to the right of the road in single file. Nothing else ranks in importance with this golden rule. It maximizes your chance of staying out of trouble every moment of every ride.

A Note about Cycling Behaviour

Today, governments at all levels have done much in the way of providing more cycle paths and dedicated routes in order to encourage cycling. As a result, many more cyclists are on the roads, trails and dyke paths than when we wrote the first edition of *Easy Cycling around Vancouver*. Fortunately for cyclists in general, the effect has been a greater awareness of the benefits of cycling and the rights of cyclists.

Unfortunately, however, letters to the editor printed in newspapers indicate that some other road users and pedestrians are becoming increasingly irritated by the dangerous riding habits and discourtesy of a few cyclists. In order to curb this growing hostility, we must act positively to build and maintain goodwill among cyclists, pedestrians and drivers. We make this appeal to our readers: Please ride with consideration toward others. *Be a responsible road user.*

> 1 PARADISE VALLEY

Squamish

. . . . .

ROUND TRIP	17 km (10 ½ miles)
TERRAIN	Paved roads; some flat, some gentle hills
TRAFFIC VOLUME	Low on Paradise Valley Road, moderate around Hwy 99
ALLOW	1 ½ to 2 ½ hours
HIGHLIGHTS	Quiet roads, mountain views, Cheakamus River, old-growth cedar
PICNIC SPOT	Dyke near Cheakamus River bridge at 8.5 km
STARTING POINT	Alice Lake Provincial Park beach and picnic area parking lot
HOW TO GET THERE	BY CAR: Leave Hwy 99 North at Alice Lake sign, 10 km north of Squamish.
	BY TRANSIT: There is no convenient transit option at this time.
WHEN TO GO	Swim at Alice Lake in July and August.

CAMPING AT Alice Lake? For a change of pace from exploring the park trails, try this short foray into secluded Paradise Valley.

After crossing the Cheakamus River in Cheekye, the road winds through typical coastal forest, much of it environmental reserve. Along the way, watch for an unobtrusive sign leading to a thousand-year-old western red cedar a few metres from the road. A boardwalk protects the base of this living giant.

A good picnic spot and turnaround point presents itself just beyond the second bridge at 8.5 kilometres, where an information

Cheakamus River

kiosk describes the formation and action of glaciers, rivers and
volcanoes. Below the dyke, the Cheakamus River sweeps around a
gravel bar.

Squamish Valley Road west of Cheekye also offers easy cycling
with breathtaking views of the Tantalus Range. River access is
limited, however, as the road runs through Squamish First Nation
reserves.

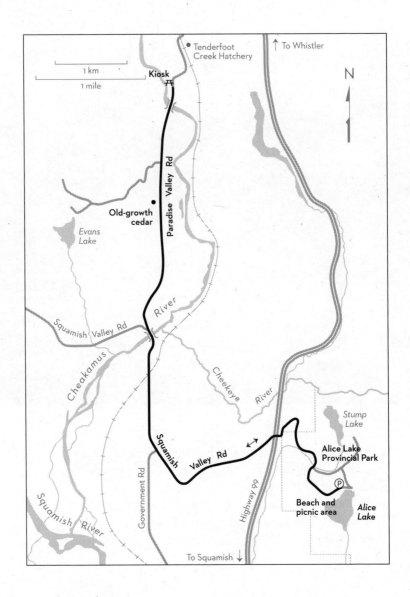

0.0   Alice Lake beach and picnic area parking lot. Proceed down the park access road to Hwy 99.

1.7   Cross Hwy 99 onto Squamish Valley Road toward Cheekye.

5.3   Cross the Cheakamus River bridge at Cheekye and immediately take the right fork onto Paradise Valley Road.

6.7   The boardwalk to the old-growth cedar is on your left.

Keep straight on past North Vancouver Outdoor School and the road to Evans Lake.

8.5   Bridge across the Cheakamus River. The information kiosk and picnic spot are ahead on your left.

OPTION: For a self-guided tour of Tenderfoot Creek Fish Hatchery, continue north for less than 2 km and turn right at the hatchery sign.

8.5   From the picnic spot, return south on Paradise Valley Road.

11.7   Left on Squamish Valley Road to cross the river in Cheekye.

17.0   Alice Lake beach and picnic area parking lot.

> 2 BRACKENDALE

Squamish

. . . . .

ROUND TRIP	19.2 km (12 miles)
TERRAIN	Paved roads; flat
TRAFFIC VOLUME	Low except around Hwy 99
ALLOW	2 to 3 hours
HIGHLIGHTS	Squamish Adventure Centre, Brackendale Eagles Provincial Park, Brackendale Art Gallery, West Coast Railway Heritage Park, Squamish River, mountain views
PICNIC SPOT	Fisherman's Park at the end of Brennan Road at 8.8 km
STARTING POINT	Visitor Information Centre (Squamish Adventure Centre) on Loggers Lane
HOW TO GET THERE	BY CAR: From Hwy 99 North turn right (east) at the Cleveland Avenue traffic lights, then immediately left onto Loggers Lane. The visitor centre is a short distance ahead; park in the gravel parking lot opposite the centre.
	BY TRANSIT: If you are already in Squamish, take Squamish Transit Route 1: Brackendale bus to Cleveland at Buckley and ride to the starting point.
WHEN TO GO	Attend the Squamish Days Loggers Sports Festival in late July or early August or view the bald eagles in winter.

Visitor centre, Squamish

SQUAMISH LIES at the foot of a granitic monolith, at the confluence of three major rivers and at the head of a fjord. The rugged landscape, a mecca for mountain bikers and rock climbers, might seem daunting to the cyclist looking for "easy" routes, but there are quiet, level roads through the Squamish/Mamquam flood plain that provide peaceful riding with mountain views.

Breeze out to Brackendale, the notorious "squamish" wind at your back, pausing at Eagle Run, where from November to February each year thousands of bald eagles gather to feed on spawned-out salmon. On the dyke, a log shelter decorated by Sko-mish First Nation carvers houses interpretive panels on eagle lore.

Perhaps eight thousand years ago, the ancestors of this region's Sko-mish people arrived at Howe Sound at the end of an unimaginable journey from Asia by way of the Bering Strait, Alaska and the northwest coast of British Columbia. Millennia later came explorers, fur traders and gold seekers and, eventually, non-Native settlers to make their home in the valley.

If you're staying in Squamish and fancy a day out of the saddle, you could explore the network of walking trails around the estuary or visit West Coast Railway Heritage Park, now the home of B.C. Rail's *Royal Hudson* steam train as well as Canada's largest collection of rolling stock. The spectacular Squamish Adventure Centre on Loggers Lane offers a café, gift shop and theatre in addition to leaflets and maps and, of course, staff on hand to answer questions.

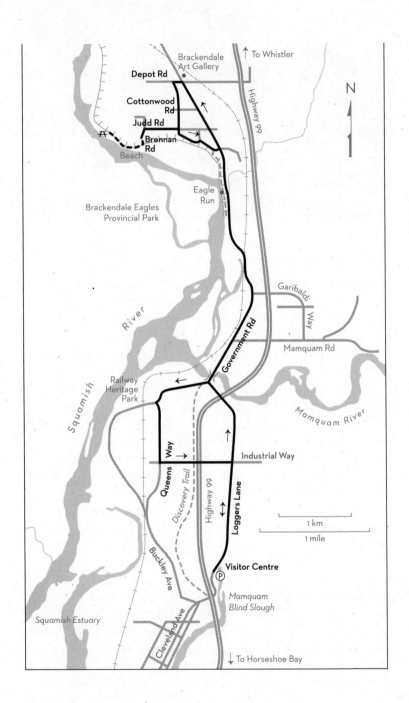

0.0   Squamish Adventure Centre parking area. Cycle north on Loggers Lane.

2.4   Bear left at the stop sign onto Centennial Way and continue through the Hwy 99 underpass.

3.0   Right on Government Road to cross the Mamquam River bridge.

5.6   Eagle-viewing area. The log shelter is on the dyke. Brackendale Eagles Provincial Park is opposite, across the Squamish River.

7.1   Brackendale Store and Café is on your left.

7.4   Left on Depot Road. To visit the Brackendale Art Gallery, continue a few metres farther on Government Road and look for the unicorn.

7.5   Left on Cottonwood Road.

8.1   Right on Judd Road.

8.6   Left on Brennan Road at the sign "River Access."

8.8   Fisherman's Park parking area. From the dyke top, a track left leads down to a sandy beach.

8.8   Backtrack on Brennan Road and turn right on Judd Road.

11.3   Right on Maple Crescent.

11.6   Right on Eagle Run Drive.

11.9   Right on Government Road.

15.2   Cross the Mamquam River bridge and go right on Government Road.

16.0   Left on Aspen Road and immediately right on Queens Way. To visit the Railway Heritage Park, continue 0.4 km farther on Government Road and turn right at the sign.

17.0   Left on Industrial Way. Cross Hwy 99.

17.9   Right on Loggers Lane.

19.2   Visitor Information Centre parking area.

> 3 SEYMOUR VALLEY TRAILWAY

Lower Seymour Conservation Reserve, North Vancouver

. . . . .

ROUND TRIP	24 km (15 miles)
TERRAIN	Paved cycle path and short unpaved trail; some hills
TRAFFIC VOLUME	Only hikers, runners, in-line skaters and other cyclists
ALLOW	3 to 4 hours
HIGHLIGHTS	Coastal forest, wildlife, river and mountain views, Seymour River Fish Hatchery, Old Growth Trail (optional)
PICNIC SPOT	Seymour River Fish Hatchery at 12 km or a picnic site along the way
STARTING POINT	Lower Seymour Conservation Reserve parking lot (Rice Lake Gate)
HOW TO GET THERE	BY CAR: Leave Hwy 1 in North Vancouver at exit 22B and drive north on Lillooet Road to its end at the Lower Seymour Conservation Reserve parking area.
	BY TRANSIT: As counterintuitive as it sounds, take the bus to Lynn Headwaters Regional Park, turn east from the bus stop and cross the pipe bridge over Lynn Creek to reach the Lower Seymour Conservation Reserve.
WHEN TO GO	Ride a shady trail on a hot summer's day.

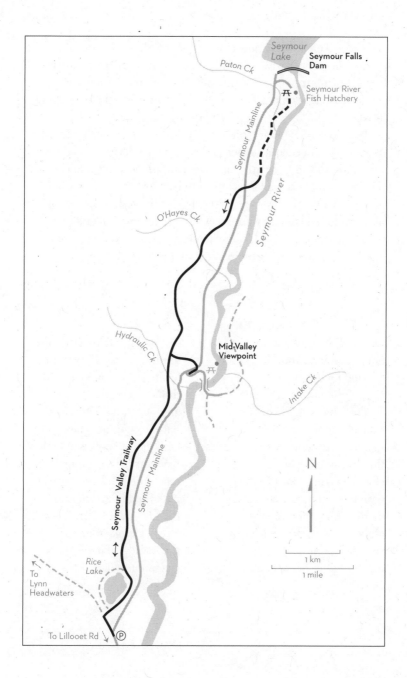

Seymour
Lake

Seymour Falls
Dam

Paton Ck

Seymour River
Fish Hatchery

Seymour Mainline

O'Hayes Ck

Seymour River

Hydraulic Ck

Mid-Valley
Viewpoint

Intake Ck

N

Seymour Valley Trailway

Seymour Mainline

1 km

1 mile

To
Lynn
Headwaters

Rice
Lake

To Lillooet Rd   P

T IS a rare pleasure to ride a bicycle (comfortably) into a wilderness area where forest, river, mountain and wildlife are close at hand. The Seymour Valley Trailway travels 12 kilometres into the glacier-carved Seymour River Valley, crossing several creeks along its way.

The Lower Seymour Conservation Reserve is a working forest in what was once closed watershed land. Since being opened for recreation in 1987, the area has been carefully managed to ensure the water supply is available for future use, if that should become necessary. The area is largely second-growth forest; remnants of old corduroy roads and wooden pipelines attest to earlier logging operations. The reserve is home to deer, bears, cougars and other animals. It is always a thrill to encounter wildlife, but play safe by keeping your distance.

THE ROUTE

Detailed instructions are not necessary: From the parking lot, head for the start of the Seymour Valley Trailway (near the Learning Lodge) and follow it for 12 kilometres to its end at the Seymour River Fish Hatchery—or as far as you wish to go. There are several picnic sites (and outhouses) along the way, as well as a 400-metre connecting trail to Mid-Valley Viewpoint.

At about 9.5 kilometres, the Trailway crosses Seymour Mainline and after a short distance continues for another 2 kilometres as a narrow, winding gravel trail with picnic spots beside the Seymour River. Those who reach the fish hatchery can park their bikes and walk the Old Growth Trail beside Hurry Creek. Your return to the LSCR parking lot is by the same route.

> 4 BURNABY TRAILS

Burnaby

· · · · ·

ROUND TRIP	14.8 km (9 ¼ miles)
TERRAIN	Paved roads and pathways, unpaved trail; some hills
TRAFFIC VOLUME	Low to moderate; some busy intersections
ALLOW	1 ½ to 2 ½ hours
HIGHLIGHTS	Confederation Park, Burnaby Mountain Urban Trail, mountain and city views
PICNIC SPOT	Confederation Park at 6.5 km
STARTING POINT	Street parking on Shellmont Street
HOW TO GET THERE	BY CAR: From Lougheed Highway (Hwy 7), turn north on Lake City Way, which becomes Arden Avenue. Turn right on Shellmont Street and park on the gravel shoulder.
	BY TRANSIT: Take SkyTrain to Lake City Way and ride to the starting point or ride the bus to Arden Avenue at Meadowood Drive.
WHEN TO GO	Early spring before foliage hides the view across Burrard Inlet.

THIS SHORT but moderately demanding ride enables you to sample some of the trails and bikeways now available to cyclists and walkers in and around the city. After a peaceful beginning along the tree-lined Burnaby Mountain Urban Trail, you switch to a signed route along a residential street—the Frances-Union Bikeway—before joining the Trans Canada Trail through the woods above Burrard Inlet. Confederation Park offers picnic tables and other facilities, if you're ready for a break before continuing the circuit via Carleton Street, which is part of the Sea to River Bikeway, and Frances-Union.

Although more urban than most of our routes, you'll quickly come to appreciate the preferential treatment accorded to cyclists on the bikeways. Obey any special directives for cyclists at intersections and, of course, all traffic signs and rules of the road. Be sure to look up now and then to catch views of the North Shore Mountains and the city around you. You can hardly miss the Viking head on Hammarskjold Drive; this giant statue with the horned helmet represents Burnaby North Secondary School's mascot and was built by students in the welding class.

KM THE ROUTE

0.0 Shellmont Street. Cross Arden Avenue and cycle right (north) on the paved Burnaby Mountain Urban Trail. Follow BMUT signs.

1.5 Cross Duthie Avenue.

2.2 Left on Union Street. Follow Frances-Union Bikeway signs. Cross Kensington Avenue at the traffic lights onto Hammarskjold Drive. Burnaby North Secondary School is on your left. At the end of Hammarskjold, continue on the paved pathway, bearing left.

3.7 Right on Fell Avenue to cross Hastings Street at the crosswalk. Continue north on Fell.

4.4 Left onto the Trans Canada Trail/Burnaby Scenic Trail at the end of Fell. Ups and downs. Use extreme caution, especially downhill on loose gravel. Watch for pedestrians and other cyclists.

5.9 Left onto Penzance Drive.

6.5 Confederation Park is on your left. Picnic tables, toilets.

6.5 Continue west on Penzance Drive, following TCT/Heights Trail signs.

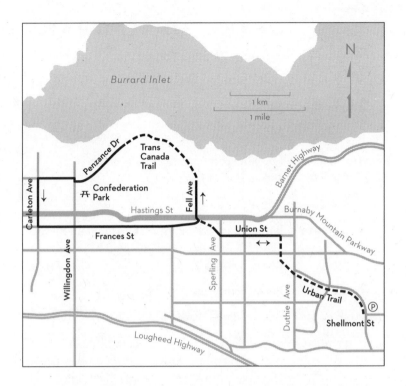

6.8 Right on Willingdon
Avenue, then immediately
left on Cambridge Street.

7.5 Left on Carleton Avenue,
following the Sea to River
Bikeway.

8.1 Cross Hastings Street
at the crosswalk.

8.3 Left on Frances Street.
Follow Frances-Union
Bikeway signs. Hills.

10.9 Left on Fell Avenue. Follow
the paved pathway east
alongside Hastings
Street, bearing right to
rejoin Hammarskjold Drive
and retrace your outward
route along Union Street.

After crossing Cliff Avenue,
remember to turn right onto
Burnaby Mountain Urban
Trail at 12.6 km.

14.8 Shellmont Street.

> 5 BARNET-INLET TRAILS

Burnaby/Port Moody

. . . . .

ROUND TRIP	15.6 km (9 ¾ miles)
TERRAIN	Unpaved trail and paved road; some hills
TRAFFIC VOLUME	Low, except moderate in Port Moody and on Barnet Highway
ALLOW	2 ½ to 3 ½ hours
HIGHLIGHTS	Barnet Marine Park, Burnaby Mountain Bicycle Skills Facility, Inlet Trail, old Port Moody town, Rocky Point Park
PICNIC SPOT	Rocky Point Park at 7.8 km
STARTING POINT	Barnet Marine Park parking lot
HOW TO GET THERE	BY CAR: From Hastings Street in Burnaby, turn left onto Inlet Drive, which becomes Barnet Highway. Turn left at the traffic lights into Barnet Marine Park parking lot.
	BY TRANSIT: Take the bus to Barnet Highway at 8300 block.
WHEN TO GO	Summer to swim at Barnet Marine Park or spring to see purple martins at Rocky Point Park.
CONNECTS WITH	Sasamat Lake, page 38

IF YOU like off-road riding with some ups and downs, this jaunt along the north slope of Burnaby Mountain to the waterfront at Port Moody is full of interest.

From the Bicycle Skills Park—don't miss the metal sculpture called "Free Rider"—you head east on the roller-coaster Barnet Trail. Stay with the powerline right-of-way, taking extreme care on

"Free Rider"

the steep descent to the road. It's better to walk your bike than lose control on loose gravel.

Along the Trans Canada Trail section known as Inlet Trail, Discovery panels describe the history and business of the inlet. You might see the Pacific Coast Terminals' giant shiploader at work beside the sulphur piles.

After a final stretch of road among the old houses and funky shops of Port Moody's old town, you can take a break in Rocky Point Park before setting off on your way back. You can retrace your outward route, but most will prefer to take advantage of the wide cycle lane on the Barnet Highway for an easier return. Finally, round off the day's outing with a stroll or swim in Barnet Marine Park. There's a waterfront walk with charming bird sculptures and views across Burrard Inlet. The park is a great place to spot seals and seabirds and to watch freighters glide by.

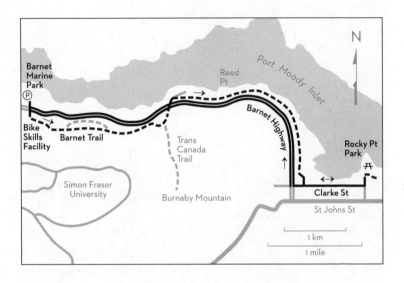

KM **THE ROUTE**

0.0 Barnet Marine Park parking
lot. Cross Barnet Highway at
the traffic lights and enter
Burnaby Mountain Bicycle
Skills Facility. Stay outside
the fence enclosing the
bike park.

0.6 Go through the green gate
onto Barnet Trail.

0.9 Pass the western end of
Hang Your Hat loop trail.
Continue along the
power line.

2.0 Left on Cougar Creek Trail.
Steep downhill. Use extreme
caution, walking your bike if
necessary.

2.5 Left at the junction with
the Trans Canada Trail.
There is a kiosk with a map
here. Loose gravel. Walk
your bike down to Barnet
Highway.

2.8 Cross Barnet Highway at
the traffic lights and go
down the private Petrocan
Port road.

3.3 Right onto Trans Canada
Trail (Inlet Trail). This
narrow path, easy to miss,
is marked with a TCT sign
and an arrow affixed to a
lamppost just before the
road curves left.

3.9 There is a viewing platform on your left.

4.2 Reed Point Marina is on your left. Café, toilets. Continue uphill on the paved road.

4.5 Cross the road to resume along the Inlet Trail at the TCT sign. Watch for loose gravel. Discovery panels describe the natural and human history of the area. Continue past the sulphur piles and the Reichhold plant.

6.3 Stay left on the pavement at Short Street, which becomes Douglas Street. Andrés Wines is on your right.

6.5 Left on Clarke Street into Old Port Moody.

7.4 Left onto the overpass (Moody Street) at the traffic lights. Use the sidewalk so as not to miss the sharp right turn down the ramp to Rocky Point Park.

7.8 Rocky Point Park. Picnic tables, pier, toilets, fish and chips, ice cream.

7.8 Retrace your outward route via the overpass and Clarke Street. If you intend to return along Inlet and Barnet Trails, go right on Douglas Street. Otherwise continue on Clarke Street.

9.4 Right on Barnet Highway at the traffic lights. Cruise along in the cycle lane to Barnet Marine Park.

15.6 Barnet Marine Park parking lot. Lock up your bike and walk across the railway bridge into the park.

> 6 SASAMAT LAKE

Port Moody/Anmore

· · · · ·

ROUND TRIP	Up to 18 km (11 ¼ miles)
TERRAIN	Paved roads and cycle path; some flat, some hills
TRAFFIC VOLUME	Low to moderate
ALLOW	2 to 3 ½ hours
HIGHLIGHTS	Rocky Point Park and Station Museum, Shoreline Park, views of Burrard Inlet, Noons Creek Hatchery, Old Orchard Park, Sasamat Lake
PICNIC SPOT	White Pine Beach at 9.0 km (or Old Orchard Park on either the outward or the return leg)
STARTING POINT	Rocky Point Park in Port Moody
HOW TO GET THERE	BY CAR: From St. Johns Street in Port Moody, turn left on Moody Street. Follow the overpass around to the left and turn left onto Murray Street. The parking lot for Rocky Point Park is just beyond the Station Museum. Note that there is a 4-hour parking limit.
	BY TRANSIT: Take the West Coast Express to Port Moody Station, or take the 97 B-Line or a local bus to St. Johns Street at Williams Street.
WHEN TO GO	July and August to swim at White Pine Beach.
CONNECTS WITH	Barnet-Inlet Trails, page 34

PORT MOODY'S designated bike routes, which wind among the rolling hills surrounding Port Moody Inlet, by their very nature will take your breath away. By beginning with the gentle 3-kilometre cycle path in Shoreline Park, you have the option of turning around at the end of Alderside Road or Ioco School or simply lazing away the day in Old Orchard Park. Or you can accept the challenge and reap the reward of a picnic at Sasamat Lake, with the bonus of some freewheeling on the way home.

Shoreline Park is a precious stretch of waterfront preserved for recreational use—a commendable feat in a development-crazed society. A trail and boardwalks for pedestrians hug the shoreline. Running roughly parallel to the pedestrian trail, the cycle path passes through coniferous forest and mixed woodland with occasional views of the tidal flats. Cyclists can walk their bikes down to the mouth of Noons Creek, where unearthed middens indicate this area was once the site of Native encampments. There are glimpses of Burrard Inlet from Alderside Road, albeit from between waterfront homes.

Sasamat Lake, in Belcarra Regional Park, is often thronged on summer weekends when families come out to picnic and swim at White Pine Beach or hike the 3-kilometre trail around the lake. At other times you may find yourself with only the birds and squirrels for company.

KM   THE ROUTE

0.0   Parking lot for Rocky Point Park. Pick up the designated cycle path and proceed in an easterly direction. Side trails lead to Noons Creek Hatchery, Old Mill site and viewing platform.

3.0   Old Orchard Park. Picnic tables, toilets, beach.

Continue west along Alderside Road.

4.8   Left onto Ioco Road. Some gentle ups and downs.

5.6   Right on 1st Avenue, opposite the church. Ioco School is on the corner. Begin a gradual climb.

6.4   Keep left on Bedwell Bay Road toward Belcarra where Sunnyside Road forks right. There are some bends and steep hills but also a wide shoulder to cycle on.

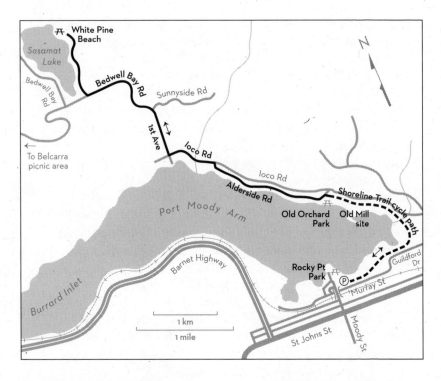

7.8 Right to White Pine Beach. Ride the gentle downhill to the beach.

9.0 Left into the first parking lot and walk bikes down the trail to the beach. Picnic tables, toilets, swimming, concession on summer weekends.

9.0 Retrace your outward route via Bedwell Bay Road, 1st Avenue, Ioco Road, Alderside Road and the Shoreline Park cycle path.

18.0 Rocky Point Park. Picnic area, toilets, pier. The Station Museum records Port Moody's railway history.

Old Orchard Park

Freighter in Burrard Inlet

> 7 COQUITLAM RIVER

Port Coquitlam/Coquitlam

. . . . .

ROUND TRIP	14.2 km (9 miles)
TERRAIN	Paved roads and pathways and unpaved trail; mostly flat
TRAFFIC VOLUME	Low, except around Pipeline Road
ALLOW	2 to 3 hours
HIGHLIGHTS	Coquitlam River, woodland trail, Town Centre Park, Lafarge Lake
PICNIC SPOT	Lafarge Lake at 7.6 km
STARTING POINT	The Red Bridge parking area on Pitt River Road
HOW TO GET THERE	BY CAR: Leave Hwy 1 at exit 44 and take Lougheed Highway (Hwy 7) east. Turn right onto Pitt River Road and cross the Red Bridge over Coquitlam River. The entrance to the parking area is on the left just beyond the east end of the bridge.
	BY TRANSIT: Take the bus to Lougheed Highway (Hwy 7) at Pitt River Road and ride to the starting point.
WHEN TO GO	May and June to see the river at its best and wildflowers beside the trail.
CONNECTS WITH	Traboulay PoCo Trail, page 46

T HIS EASY family ride follows the Coquitlam River upstream, skirting two neighbourhood parks before entering tranquil woodland.

The river is clear and shallow, occasionally frothing into white water as it flows southward from Coquitlam Lake reservoir to feed the Pitt River. Its surroundings are the traditional territory of Kwikwetlem First Nation. Today, trusty Trans Canada Trail signs temporarily divert wayfarers from the river and into Coquitlam's well-appointed Town Centre Park—a reclaimed quarry site with various sports fields, tennis courts and an artificial lake stocked with trout for public fishing. The 1.25-kilometre Lakeside Loop Trail is popular with walkers and joggers; a sign requests that cyclists "Go slow and keep to the right."

KM **THE ROUTE**

0.0 The Red Bridge parking area.

Locate the Traboulay PoCo Trail sign at the east end of the parking lot and set off on the wide paved pathway. Entering Gates Park, cycle around the sports field and follow Traboulay PoCo Trail as it passes beneath Kingsway and the railway.

2.6 Enter Lions Park. Still following Traboulay PoCo Trail, pass beneath Lougheed Highway and continue on the gravel path beside the river.

3.8 Cross the blue footbridge at the end of Patricia Avenue, switching from the Traboulay PoCo Trail to the Trans Canada Trail, and turn right to continue along the west side of the river.

4.7 Keep right, following TCT signs. Trails to the left lead to neighbourhood streets.

6.0 Trans Canada Trail leaves the river. Go left along the lane.

6.4 Left onto Gabriola Drive. Watch for TCT sign on your right, opposite Nestor Street. Take this short path between houses to emerge on David Avenue. Go left and use the pedestrian crossing to cross Pipeline Road at the traffic light.

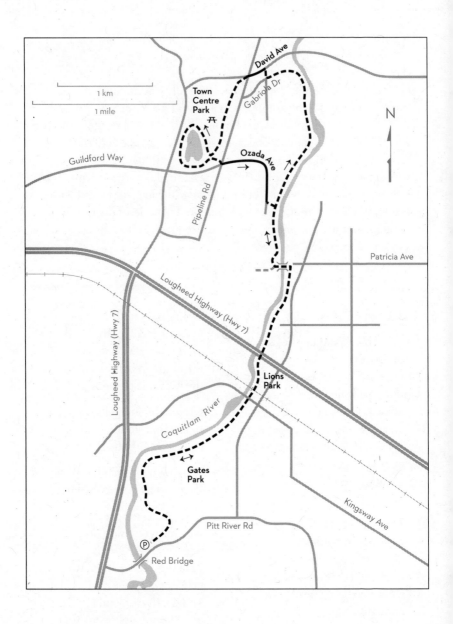

6.6 Enter Town Centre Park and go left on the paved pathway. Follow TCT signs past sports fields and a parking lot. (There are public toilets in the building beside the tennis courts.)

7.6 Trans Canada Trail pavilion at the eastern end of Lafarge Lake. Benches and picnic tables overlook the lake.

7.6 To continue, follow TCT signs north along the lakeshore, then continue south on the Lakeside Loop Trail where the Trans Canada Trail diverges west to Douglas College campus.

8.3 Keep right on the paved pathway where a gravel trail branches left along the lakeshore, then go left onto the multi-use pathway beside Guildford Way.

8.5 Left at the fork.

8.6 At the TCT pavilion, head uphill, away from the lake.

8.8 Intersection of Pipeline Road and Guildford Way. Cross at the pedestrian crossing and cycle downhill on Ozada Avenue.

9.3 Left at the wide gravel parking space. Cross the bridge, pass the playground and keep right to rejoin the Coquitlam River trail.

9.3 Retrace your outward route, re-crossing the blue footbridge at 10.4 km to follow Traboulay PoCo Trail back to your starting point.

14.2 The Red Bridge parking area.

> 8 TRABOULAY POCO TRAIL

Coquitlam/Port Coquitlam

. . . . .

ROUND TRIP	24.8 km (15 ½ miles)
TERRAIN	Unpaved trail and dyke and paved roads; mostly flat
TRAFFIC VOLUME	Low
ALLOW	3 to 4 hours
HIGHLIGHTS	Colony Farm Regional Park, Coquitlam River, Gates and Lions Parks, urban forest, Hyde Creek Nature Reserve, De Boville Slough, Pitt River
PICNIC SPOT	There are benches along the dyke after 12.8 km
STARTING POINT	Shaughnessy Street parking lot
HOW TO GET THERE	BY CAR: From Mary Hill Bypass in Coquitlam turn south on Shaughnessy Street at the traffic lights. The parking area is just around the bend.
	BY TRANSIT: Catch the West Coast Express to Port Coquitlam Station and ride to the starting point or take the bus to Shaughnessy at Mary Hill Bypass.
WHEN TO GO	Spring or fall to see the Colony Farm lands at their best.
CONNECTS WITH	Coquitlam River, page 42; De Boville Slough, page 50

Pitt River

A LTHOUGH SECTIONS of the Traboulay PoCo Trail are included
in other rides (see Coquitlam River and De Boville Slough),
it would be a pity not to include the entire circular route
in this book.

The brainchild of Pitt River swing-bridge operator Harold
Routley, the idea of a trail that would encircle the City of Port
Coquitlam captured the imagination of the community. The
trail was completed in 1974, its maintenance turned over to Port
Coquitlam Parks and Recreation soon after. More recently, the trail
was renamed in honour of the late mayor, Len Traboulay.

Improvements and changes to the trail continue to be made
when necessary—at the time of writing, there is a temporary
detour because of construction around the Pitt River Bridge; also,

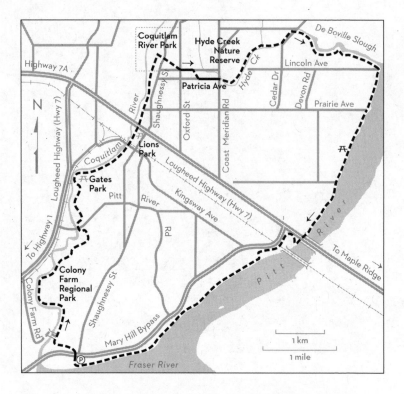

deterioration of a trail in Colony Farm lands has resulted in an agreement with the Kwikwetlem to divert the route through their reserve.

The Traboulay PoCo Trail is here to stay. Cyclists and walkers need only follow the trail signs to make a unique journey beside rivers and creeks, through urban forest and neighbourhood parks. Note that the shared trail is very popular, especially on weekends; please cycle safely and be courteous to other users.

0.0 Shaughnessy Street parking area. Turn right from the parking lot and cross Mary Hill Bypass at the traffic lights. Look for the PoCo Trail sign on the west side of Shaughnessy Street.

1.3 Millennium Bridge, Colony Farm Regional Park. Continue on the east side of Coquitlam River.

3.1 Left through the wire gate.

4.2 Pitt River Road. There is no road crossing—follow PoCo Trail signs left and through the underpass. Continue across the Red Bridge parking lot onto the paved pathway. Follow the path around the perimeter of Gates Park.

6.5 Go through the Kingsway and the railway underpasses.

6.9 Lions Park. Picnic tables, toilets. Pass beneath Lougheed Highway.

8.3 Pass beneath the Patricia Avenue footbridge. Keep a keen eye out for PoCo Trail signs in this forested section. Watch out for other cyclists, too.

9.2 Cross Shaughnessy Street and follow PoCo Trail signs along neighbourhood trails and streets.

10.6 Cross Coast Meridian Road. Enter Hyde Creek Nature Reserve.

12.8 De Boville Slough parking area. Continue along the dyke path on the south side of the slough.

18.5 Lougheed Highway and Pitt River Bridge. Follow PoCo and other signs for bicycles through the temporary detour, until you are back on the dyke path south of the bridge.

24.8 Shaughnessy Street parking lot.

> 9 DE BOVILLE SLOUGH

Coquitlam/Port Coquitlam

. . . . .

ROUND TRIP	17.2 km (10 ¾ miles)
TERRAIN	Paved roads, gravel dyke paths and trail; flat
TRAFFIC VOLUME	Low, except on Prairie Avenue
ALLOW	2 to 3 hours
HIGHLIGHTS	Pitt River, De Boville Slough, Minnekhada Regional Park, Hyde Creek and PoCo Trails
PICNIC SPOT	Minnekhada Regional Park at 10.5 km or Addington Lookout
STARTING POINT	Cedar Drive Park on Prairie Avenue
HOW TO GET THERE	BY CAR: From Lougheed Highway (Hwy 7), drive north on Coast Meridian Road. Turn right on Prairie Avenue and drive for about 1 km to the small park on the right.
	BY TRANSIT: Catch the West Coast Express to Port Coquitlam Station and/or take the bus to Prairie Avenue at Cedar Drive.
WHEN TO GO	Look for spawning salmon in Hyde Creek in September.
CONNECTS WITH	Traboulay PoCo Trail, page 46

TEN KILOMETRES of dyke top and trail help to make this a safe and interesting family ride. The circuit is short, but there is much to see and do. Budding naturalists will spot herons and waterfowl in the marshes bordering De Boville Slough, ospreys over the Pitt River and muskrats sliding into the water from their muddy holes. In September, you might see chum salmon heading up the slough to spawn in Hyde Creek. Binoculars are useful on this ride.

Pitt River

The climb to Addington Lookout could be a popular option, rewarding the energetic with a grand view across Addington Marsh and the Pitt River to the Golden Ears. For a less challenging lunch spot, wheel into Minnekhada Regional Park, where picnic tables and other facilities are at hand. Hiking trails encircle the marsh and ascend the park's two rocky knolls. Minnekhada Lodge, once part of the private domain of B.C.'s lieutenant governors, is open to the public most Sunday afternoons.

After a short stretch on Cedar Drive the route joins Hyde Creek Trail, part of the PoCo Trail system encompassing the area between the Coquitlam and Pitt Rivers. Cycling the wide gravel track through stately forest, you'll reach the Hyde Creek Recreation Centre—a mere 1.3 kilometres from your starting point on Prairie Avenue.

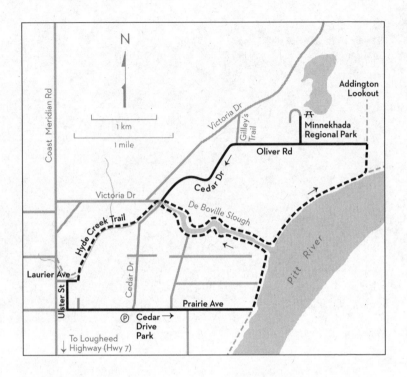

KM THE ROUTE

0.0 Cedar Drive Park. Right (east) on Prairie Avenue.

2.1 Left onto dyke path. Cycle first along Pitt River then along De Boville Slough.

5.2 Turn right on Cedar Drive and right again onto the path on the north bank of De Boville Slough. The path veers away from the water then continues along Pitt River.

9.1 Left after the farm and continue straight ahead toward Minnekhada hill.

9.5 OPTION: Straight ahead on the dyke leads to a footpath up to Addington Lookout. Lock your bicycle before climbing. Otherwise, go left at the gate onto Oliver Road.

10.2 Right between gateposts to Minnekhada Regional Park.

10.5 Bend in driveway: picnic tables, bike rack, toilets. Minnekhada Lodge is up the hill at end of the driveway.

10.5 Return along the driveway.

10.8 Right on Oliver Road. Minnekhada Farm is on the right, now being restored. There is currently no access to the farm. Keep straight ahead on Cedar Drive.

13.8 De Boville Slough gate. Go straight across the intersection onto the signposted Hyde Creek Trail.

After the bridge, continue right on PoCo Trail.

15.9 Hyde Creek Recreation Centre parking lot. Head left past the recreation centre building to join Laurier Avenue then left onto Ulster Street.

16.5 Left on Prairie Avenue. Use the crosswalk at this intersection if necessary.

17.2 Cedar Drive Park.

> 10 IONA ISLAND

Richmond

. . . . .

ROUND TRIP	18.7 km (11 ½ miles)
TERRAIN	Paved road and unpaved service road; flat
TRAFFIC VOLUME	Low
ALLOW	1 ½ to 2 ½ hours
HIGHLIGHTS	Ocean and river views, beach, Iona jetty, McDonald Beach Park
PICNIC SPOT	Iona Beach Regional Park at 13.4 km
STARTING POINT	McDonald Beach Park
HOW TO GET THERE	BY CAR: From Grant McConachie Way (the approach road to Vancouver Airport's main terminal) turn right on Templeton Street, left on Grauer Road and right on McDonald Road.
	BY TRANSIT: Take the Canada Line SkyTrain to Templeton Station and ride to the starting point.
WHEN TO GO	Watch for migratory birds in spring and fall.

F OR MANY urban cyclists, a quick way to get out in the open with a bike is to skirt Vancouver Airport and head for Iona Island. Some may be able to cycle from home to this destination, or transport their bicycles by car, bus or SkyTrain as far as Templeton Street, just off Grant McConachie Way. For the short and easy ride described here, a convenient place to start and finish is McDonald Beach Park, which offers shaded picnic tables on the riverbank and lively boating activity to watch.

Situated at the mouth of the North Arm of the Fraser River, Iona Beach Regional Park comprises riverbank, marsh, tidal flats

McDonald Beach Park

and a long sandy beach backed by grassy dunes. A service road alongside a 4-kilometre-long pipeline carrying treated sewage out to sea provides cyclists with an unusual sea-level ride with a nautical bias. Note that this is a popular training spot for road racers and rollerbladers, so keep an eye out for packs of cyclists and rollerbladers whizzing by.

Iona is an important stopover on the Pacific Flyway, attracting thousands of migrants in spring and fall and many keen birdwatchers year-round. The island is usually breezy, so make sure you have windproof clothing.

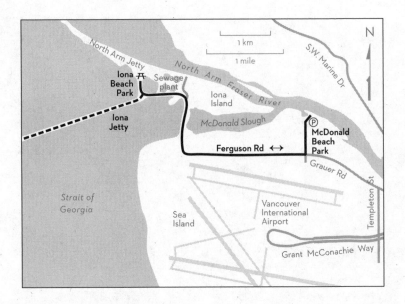

KM **THE ROUTE**

0.0 McDonald Beach Park.

0.8 Right on Ferguson Road.

3.3 Causeway linking Sea Island and Iona Island. McDonald Slough is on your right.

4.2 Left to Iona Beach Regional Park. Pipeline from sewage treatment plant alongside road.

5.1 Left on Iona jetty at the information kiosk. Cyclists must use the service road, not the walkway on top of the pipe.

9.1 Jetty terminus. View from the platform of the North Shore Mountains and Vancouver Island.

9.1 Backtrack along the jetty.

13.1 Left on road.

13.4 Parking lot and South Marsh. Toilets, beach access and picnic tables.

13.4 Retrace your outward route.

18.7 McDonald Beach Park.

> 11 TERRA NOVA CIRCUIT

Richmond

. . . . .

ROUND TRIP	21.4 km (13 ½ miles)
TERRAIN	Paved roads, unpaved trail, gravel dyke; flat
TRAFFIC VOLUME	Moderate to heavy on major roads, low elsewhere
ALLOW	2 to 3 hours
HIGHLIGHTS	Fraser River and airport activity, mountain views, Shell Road Trail, Terra Nova Waterfront Park, Terra Nova Rural Park Community Gardens, Richmond Olympic Oval
PICNIC SPOT	Terra Nova Waterfront Park at 14.8 km
STARTING POINT	Garden City Community Park or roadside parking on Granville Avenue east of the park entrance, near the tennis courts
HOW TO GET THERE	BY CAR: From Westminster Highway in Richmond, drive south to Granville Avenue. The community park is on Granville Avenue, just east of Garden City Road.
	BY TRANSIT: Take the Canada Line SkyTrain to Brighouse Station and ride to the starting point.
WHEN TO GO	See the community gardens at their best in July. Or go November to February to see snow geese from West Dyke Trail.
CONNECTS WITH	Richmond South Dyke, page 60

ON THIS circular route you'll sample some of Richmond's dedicated bicycle lanes. Be prepared to cycle with traffic on these streets; although they are designated bike routes, it's up to you to obey road signs and travel with care. By contrast, there are scenic stretches along dyke paths and on the surprisingly peaceful Shell Road Trail. From the Middle Arm Dyke Trail you can watch the constant arrivals and departures of aircraft to and from Vancouver International Airport on Sea Island and seaplane activity along the Fraser River.

The route also provides several options: Cycle the popular West Dyke Trail along the fringe of Sturgeon Bank marshes; visit a community garden where you'll see plots of vegetables and flowers and a "waterwise" demonstration garden; take a jaunt to the Richmond Olympic Oval, built to house the speed skating events of the 2010 Olympic Winter Games and now a multi-use sports facility. The fabulous building is a model of environmental design: Rainwater from the roof is collected in the pond beneath the Water Sky Garden sculpture and used for irrigation and flushing toilets; the striking heron's wing roof is made from wood salvaged from pine beetle–infested forests in the interior of British Columbia.

KM THE ROUTE

0.0 Garden City Community Park. Ride east on Granville Avenue.

1.5 Right on Shell Road Trail, just before the railway.

3.5 Continue on Shell Road.

4.4 Right on Williams Road.

9.2 Right on Railway Avenue.

OPTION: Continue for 1.8 km to the end of Williams Road, then go north on West Dyke Trail for 4 km to Terra Nova. To visit Terra Nova Rural Park Community Gardens, leave the dyke after about 3.5 km at Westminster Highway. The gardens are on the left.

11.6 Left on Granville Avenue at the traffic lights.

12.7 Right on Barnard Drive.

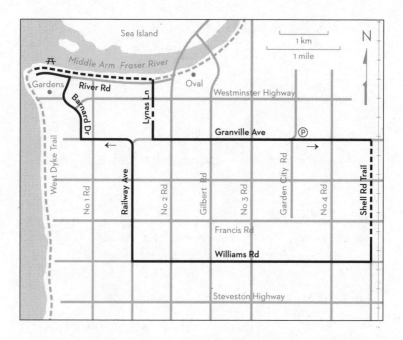

14.1 Left on River Road.

14.8 Terra Nova Waterfront Park. Picnic tables, toilets. To continue, cycle east on Middle Arm Dyke Trail.

17.3 Descend to River Road where convenient and go right on Lynas Lane, continuing through the unpaved section.

OPTION: Stay on Middle Arm Dyke Trail for another kilometre to visit Richmond Olympic Oval. Backtrack to Lynas Lane and add 2 km to subsequent distances.

18.5 Left on Granville Avenue.

21.4 Left into Garden City Community Park (or continue to roadside parking).

> 12 RICHMOND SOUTH DYKE

Richmond

. . . . .

ROUND TRIP	20.3 km (12 ¾ miles)
TERRAIN	Paved road and unpaved path; flat
TRAFFIC VOLUME	Low, except in Steveston
ALLOW	2 to 3 hours
HIGHLIGHTS	River and ocean views, Finn Slough, London Farm, Steveston wharf and village, Gulf of Georgia Cannery, Garry Point, Scotch Pond
PICNIC SPOT	Garry Point at 10.4 km
STARTING POINT	Woodwards Landing parking lot on Dyke Road
HOW TO GET THERE	BY CAR: Leave Hwy 99 at exit 32 and drive west on Steveston Highway. Turn left on No. 5 Road and right on Dyke Road. The parking area is on the right after 0.3 km.
	BY TRANSIT: Take the bus to No. 5 Road at Machrina Way and ride to the starting point.
WHEN TO GO	March to June to watch for sea lions off Garry Point and see lupines in bloom.
CONNECTS WITH	Terra Nova Circuit, page 57

THERE IS no better way to enjoy Richmond's South Dyke Trail than by bicycle. From Woodwards Landing at Horseshoe Slough Trail's eastern end to Steveston's heritage waterfront, a succession of interesting scenes and places unfold.

Fishboat in Cannery Channel

Tugs and fishboats bustle about on the south arm of the Fraser River. Finn Slough (seen on your return route) is the relic of an 1890s Finnish fishing community, its sheds and houses built on pilings. Farther west, you could visit London Farm or the Britannia Heritage Shipyard, or simply follow your nose, and South Dyke Trail signs, to Steveston village. Make your way to the public wharf to browse among gift shops, sample tasty Japanese snacks or buy fresh fish on the dock.

After gazing down at the seiners and gillnetters in the harbour, you can learn more of Steveston's fishing and canning history by touring the Gulf of Georgia Cannery, where a 1930s production line clanks through its routine. Finally, if you have not succumbed to Steveston's famous fish and chips, take your picnic lunch to Garry Point Park, sit back and contemplate the ocean, or perhaps watch kites being reeled out into the westerly breezes.

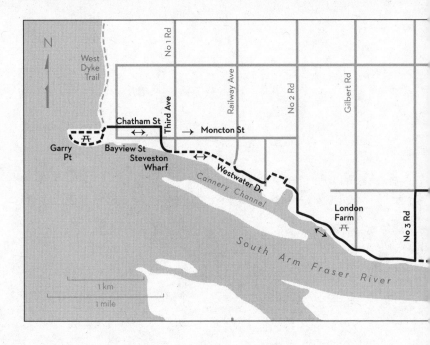

KM THE ROUTE

0.0 Woodwards Landing parking lot. Right (west) on Dyke Road.

1.6 Right on No. 4 Road for a detour through Richmond's fast-disappearing farmland.

2.5 Left on Finn Road.

4.3 Left on No. 3 Road.

5.3 Right on Dyke Road. If you choose to cycle on South Dyke Trail, please be courteous to other users.

6.5 London Farm is on your right. Continue on Dyke Road. After skirting a marina and crossing Trites Road, Dyke Road becomes Westwater Drive.

8.3 Where Westwater Drive bends into Railway Avenue, go left between the posts at the end of the parking lot. Follow this wide, paved path around a pond. (Cycling is not allowed on the boardwalk.)

8.7 Head left toward the viewing tower and cycle (slowly) west along the promenade, giving way to pedestrians.

9.2 Left onto Bayview Street. The entrance to the public wharf is on your left. Shops, restaurants, fish sales on the

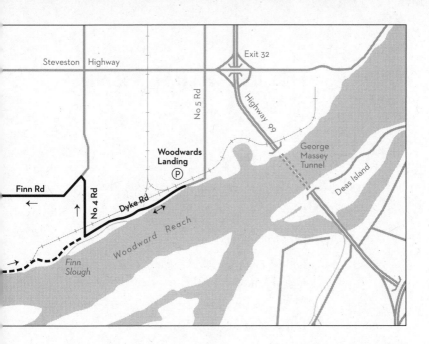

dock. Continue on Bayview
Street, which bends right
to become Third Avenue.
Cross Moncton Street.

9.8 Left on Chatham Street.

10.4 Garry Point Park. Picnic
tables, toilets, Japanese
garden, fishermen's
memorial, beaches.

Cycle (slowly) clockwise
around Garry Point for a
view of the Strait of Georgia
and fishboats in Scotch
Pond.

11.4 Go east on Chatham Street
and retrace your outward
route via Third Avenue,

Bayview Street, Westwater
Drive and Dyke Road as far
as the foot of No. 3 Road.

16.6 Go straight ahead at the gate
where No. 3 Road bends left,
into the dog off-leash area.
Follow the trail around the
Crown Packaging premises.

18.7 Gate at Finn Slough. Go
straight ahead. Buildings on
pilings, Dinner Plate Island
School, information about
Finnish settlement at the
bridge.

20.3 Woodwards Landing
parking lot.

> 13 MILLENNIUM TRAIL

Delta

· · · · ·

ROUND TRIP	12.2 km (7 ½ miles)
TERRAIN	Paved roads, gravel dyke path, trail; flat
TRAFFIC VOLUME	Low
ALLOW	1 ½ to 2 ½ hours
HIGHLIGHTS	Ladner Harbour Park, Captain's Cove Marina, Deas Island Regional Park, river traffic, waterfowl, raptors
PICNIC SPOT	Deas Island Regional Park at 6.2 km
STARTING POINT	Ladner Harbour Park
HOW TO GET THERE	BY CAR: From Vancouver, turn off Hwy 99 at exit 29 immediately south of the Massey Tunnel. Follow River Road toward Ladner for just over 2 km and turn right on McNeeley's Way at the sign to Ladner Harbour Park. From other directions, use Ladner Trunk Road (Hwy 10) and turn right on Elliott Street in Ladner and right on River Road.
	BY TRANSIT: Take the bus to Central Avenue and Ladner Trunk Road or to Ladner Exchange, or catch the bike shuttle to the south end of the George Massey Tunnel and ride to the starting point.
WHEN TO GO	Early spring when Deas Island eagles are rebuilding their nests and raising young.
CONNECTS WITH	Westham Island, page 68

Captain's Cove Marina

SINCE IT opened in 2003, Delta's Millennium Trail has been popular with walkers and cyclists. With the addition of the Deas Island Link in September 2008, trail users can now continue along the dyke between Deas Slough and adjacent farmland to enjoy the riverside picnic tables, trails and heritage buildings of Deas Island Regional Park.

Our route, perfect for cycling families, uses bike-friendly Ferry Road to join the Millennium Trail at Captain's Cove Marina. After crossing the Millennium Bridge, the trail passes beneath Hwy 99 to emerge on River Road beside the Riverhouse Pub and Restaurant. Although this establishment may tempt some travellers, most will continue along the dyke to Deas Island for a picnic beside the Fraser River where you can watch tugs, fishboats and freighters going about their business.

A plaque near the information kiosk tells of the island's first settler, tinsmith John Sullivan Deas, who built a fish cannery on the island in 1873. Park leaflets describe the history of the three heritage buildings. As you cycle inland on the main park road, look for a large eagles' nest in the bordering cottonwoods. Other trails are best explored on foot.

Our return route follows another section of the Millennium Trail beside a golf course, then takes quiet residential streets to rejoin Ferry Road.

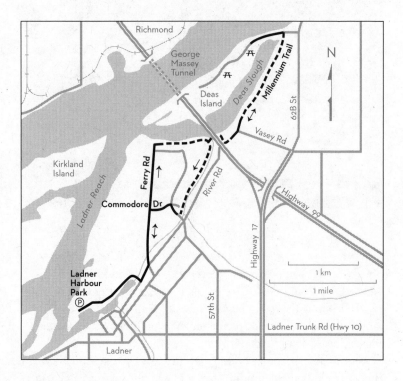

KM   THE ROUTE

0.0   Ladner Harbour Park.
Walking trails, birdwatching,
fishboats and pleasure boats
in the channel.

0.7   Left on River Road.

1.1   Left on Ferry Road at
the stop sign.

2.7   Straight ahead at the
roundabout. Pass the
boatyard and turn left beside
the Rusty Anchor Pub.

Turn right opposite the pub
entrance onto the gravel
path alongside the marina.

3.7   Walk your bike across
the bridge opposite the
Millennium Trail plaque.
Use caution as you cycle
through the underpass
beneath Hwy 99. Follow
the trail and continue on
the paved road past the
Riverhouse Restaurant
and condominiums.

4.5 At the road's end, go through the barrier onto the dyke. Along Deas Slough, watch for herons, diving birds, hawks, eagles, rowing skiffs.

5.8 Left onto Deas Island Regional Park access road.

6.2 Riverside picnic tables, toilets, viewing tower, heritage buildings, trail maps available at the information kiosk.

6.2 From Deas Island retrace your outward route through the Hwy 99 underpass.

8.7 Turn left at the Millennium Trail plaque and follow the gravel track bordering the golf course. Continue to the end, keeping the school on your right.

9.8 Right on Admiral Boulevard.

9.9 Left on Commodore Drive at the traffic light.

10.3 Left on Ferry Road.

11.1 Right on River Road.

11.5 Right on McNeeley's Way.

12.2 Ladner Harbour Park.

> 14 WESTHAM ISLAND

Delta

. . . . .

ROUND TRIP	20.5 km (12 ¾ miles)
TERRAIN	Paved roads; flat
TRAFFIC VOLUME	Low, moderate in Ladner
ALLOW	2 to 2 ½ hours
HIGHLIGHTS	Ladner Harbour Park, George C. Reifel Migratory Bird Sanctuary, berry farms, Canoe Passage, Delta Museum & Archives
PICNIC SPOT	Reifel bird sanctuary at 10.1 km
STARTING POINT	Ladner Harbour Park
HOW TO GET THERE	BY CAR: From Vancouver, turn off Hwy 99 at exit 29 immediately south of the Massey Tunnel. Follow River Road toward Ladner for just over 2 km and turn right on McNeeley's Way at the sign to Ladner Harbour Park. From other directions, use Ladner Trunk Road (Hwy 10) and turn right on Elliott Street in Ladner and right on River Road.
	BY TRANSIT: Take the bus to Central Avenue and Ladner Trunk Road or to Ladner Exchange, or catch the bike shuttle to the south end of the George Massey Tunnel and ride to the starting point.
WHEN TO GO	Sample fruit and vegetables at roadside stalls June to August.
CONNECTS WITH	Millennium Trail, page 64; Ladner Dyke, page 71

Although westham Island could be included in the Ladner Dyke ride, we present it separately because the George C. Reifel Migratory Bird Sanctuary, situated on the estuarine marsh at the mouth of the Fraser River, deserves more than a cursory visit and makes a good family outing.

Outside the entrance is a grassy picnic area, much favoured by panhandling ducks, geese and coots. The refuge is open daily, and for a modest charge you can walk (but not cycle) the 3 kilometres of pathways and visit an interpretive centre in the warming hut. A gift shop is open to all.

Thanks to its protective dykes, Westham Island is rich agricultural land growing corn, potatoes, cabbages and soft fruits. In berry season, you might be glad of a spare pannier. All-season cyclists may see flocks of over-wintering swans and snow geese feeding in the fields.

The dyke beside River Road West affords glimpses of river traffic, boatyards and floathouse living. If you'd like to see how a local household looked at the turn of the last century, visit the Delta Museum & Archives at Bridge and Delta Streets—the heart of old Ladner.

KM THE ROUTE

0.0 Ladner Harbour Park. Walking trails, birdwatching. Fishboats and pleasure boats in the channel.

0.5 Right on River Road.

1.0 Right on Elliott Street. An old government wharf lies on the corner of Chisholm Street—fish sales in season. Chisholm becomes Georgia Street.

1.5 Right on 48th Avenue.

1.9 Right on River Road West.

4.2 Wellington Point. View of Canoe Passage and Westham and Barber Islands.

4.9 Right over Westham Island Road bridge. Caution: This is a single-lane bridge with uneven boards; it is slippery when wet. Westham Island Road becomes Robertson Road.

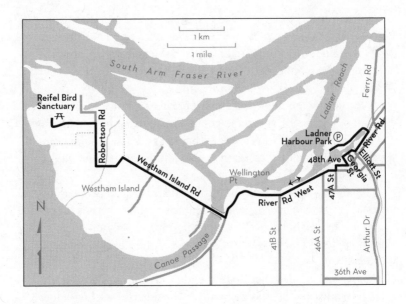

9.1 Left at the sign to George C. Reifel Migratory Bird Sanctuary.

10.1 Parking lot and entrance. Picnic tables, toilets, gift shop.

10.1 Retrace your outward route to Westham Island bridge.

15.3 Left on River Road West.

18.4 Left at 47A Street to 48th Avenue.

18.7 Left on Georgia Street, which becomes Chisholm Street.

OPTION: Go right off Chisholm onto Delta Street to visit Ladner's old town and the Delta Museum. Chisholm becomes Elliott Street.

19.6 Left on River Road.

20.0 Left on McNeeley's Way to Ladner Harbour Park.

20.5 Ladner Harbour Park parking lot.

> 15 LADNER DYKE

Delta

. . . . .

ROUND TRIP	20.9 km (13 miles)
TERRAIN	Paved roads and unpaved dyke path; flat
TRAFFIC VOLUME	Low, moderate on River Road West
ALLOW	2 ½ to 3 ½ hours
HIGHLIGHTS	Ocean and mountain views, Canoe Passage, tidal marsh
PICNIC SPOT	Below the dyke path after 10.5 km
STARTING POINT	Ladner Leisure Centre on Clarence Taylor Crescent
HOW TO GET THERE	BY CAR: From Vancouver, leave Hwy 99 south of the Massey Tunnel at exit 28. Follow Hwy 17 south for 1.5 km and turn right on Ladner Trunk Road (Hwy 10). Turn left at the next traffic light onto Harvest Drive and left again on Clarence Taylor Crescent. The Ladner Leisure Centre is on the left after the bend. From other directions, use Ladner Trunk Road (Hwy 10) to the traffic light at Harvest Drive.
	BY TRANSIT: Take the bus to Ladner Exchange or catch the bike shuttle to the south end of the George Massey Tunnel and ride to the starting point.
WHEN TO GO	View colourful marsh plants in September and October.
CONNECTS WITH	Westham Island, page 68

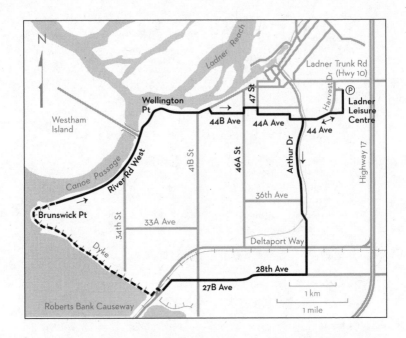

AN EASY run through the farmland south of Ladner comes to a halt at the causeway leading to Roberts Bank Superport, where long coal trains from the Kootenays and Alberta wait to be unloaded onto freighters bound for Pacific Rim countries.

Beyond the gate onto the dyke, the scene changes. Cycling the countrified dyke between fields and tidal marsh, you share the domain of herons, hawks and waterfowl. In winter, swans and snow geese can often be seen at the water's edge. Take binoculars. In late summer, carry a container for blackberries. Driftwood and sheltering bushes provide a picnic spot below the dyke, with a view across the Strait of Georgia to Vancouver Island. As you round Brunswick Point, look across the cattail marsh for some old pilings—they are the remains of one of the earliest salmon canneries in Delta.

0.0   Ladner Leisure Centre parking lot. Left on Clarence Taylor Crescent.

0.3   Right on Mountain View Boulevard.

0.6   Left on Harvest Drive, which becomes 44th Avenue.

1.7   Left on Arthur Drive at the traffic light. Arthur Drive becomes 53rd Street.

4.3   Cross Deltaport Way on the overpass.

5.0   Right on 28th Avenue, which becomes 27B Avenue.

7.4   Cross 41B Street and continue on 27B Avenue. Roberts Bank coal port ahead.

8.2   Go right across the railway tracks at the stop sign just after the bend. Caution: Trains are moved electronically, without warning.

Follow the dirt track to the left.

8.5   Right onto the dyke at the gate. Suitable lunch spots can be found a short distance north of the farm, where a path leads to a picnic table below the dyke and to driftwood along the foreshore.

11.9   After rounding Brunswick Point, you can descend to River Road West at the gate.

15.4   Wellington Point is on your left. View of Canoe Passage and Westham and Barber Islands. Watch for seals and sea lions feeding around the cannery.

17.0   Right on Church Street then left on 44B Avenue.

17.6   Left on 46A Street then immediately right on 45th Avenue.

17.8   Right on 47th Street.

18.0   Left on 44A Avenue.

18.7   Right on 50th Street.

18.8   Left on 44th Avenue.

19.3   Cross Arthur Drive at the traffic light and continue on 44th Avenue.

20.4   Right on Mountain View Boulevard.

20.7   Left on Clarence Taylor Crescent.

20.9   Ladner Leisure Centre parking lot.

> 16 **BOUNDARY BAY**

Delta

. . . .

ROUND TRIP	17.6 km (11 miles)
TERRAIN	Paved roads and gravel dyke; flat
TRAFFIC VOLUME	Low, except moderate on Boundary Bay Road
ALLOW	2 to 3 hours
HIGHLIGHTS	Ocean and mountain views; tidal flats and lagoon; raptors, shorebirds, waterfowl; Centennial Beach
PICNIC SPOT	Centennial Beach at 8.0 km
STARTING POINT	Dyke at the south foot of 72nd Street
HOW TO GET THERE	BY CAR: Leave Hwy 99, south of the Massey Tunnel, at exit 28. Follow Hwy 17 south for 1.5 km and turn left on Ladner Trunk Road (Hwy 10). Turn right on 72nd Street and proceed to its end at the dyke. Park on the wide shoulder.
	BY TRANSIT: Take the bus to 72nd Street and Churchill Street and ride to the starting point.
WHEN TO GO	March through May to see spring migratory birds; July and August to swim at Centennial Beach.
CONNECTS WITH	Mud Bay, page 78

BOUNDARY BAY is of prime importance to migratory and wintering birds hungry for the intertidal plants and animals to be found offshore and in the marsh. Flanking the entire 16-kilometre width of the bay is a gravel dyke, well used by birdwatchers, hikers, joggers and cyclists.

Observation tower, Centennial Beach

The turnaround point for this ride is Centennial Beach, abutting the U.S. border. Overlooked by Mount Baker on the eastern horizon, the beach is a great place for swimming, picnicking on the sand or beneath the trees (or at the concession) or exploring a self-guided nature trail among the dunes. Please note, though, that cycling is permitted on the multi-use 12th Avenue Dyke Trail only. Take your binoculars—there are observation towers and viewing platforms along the way.

Our route includes a diversion into the cosy community of Boundary Bay, where garden lovers can visit an unusual garden. The Secret Garden of Boundary Bay was made by a resident for the neighbourhood to enjoy. If you choose to visit, please leave your bicycle outside the garden. There is no charge for visiting, but donations are welcome.

0.0   South foot of 72nd Street. Go right onto the dyke.

4.1   Right on the footpath where the dyke ends, and continue straight ahead on 17A Avenue. Beach Grove Park is on your right.

4.6   Left on Farrell Crescent.

4.9   Right on 16th Avenue.

5.1   Left on Gillespie Road.

6.0   Left on 12th Avenue. Go through the parking lot onto the 12th Avenue Dyke Trail. Tidal lagoon and viewing platform. Follow the multi-use gravel dyke to Centennial Beach; other paths are out-of-bounds for cyclists.

8.0   Leave the park by the gate south of the concession and cycle along Centennial Parkway.

8.4   Right on 4th Avenue. To find the Secret Garden, keep straight ahead on the grassy path from the bend in the road. Otherwise, continue south on 67A Street. Cross 3rd Avenue.

9.0   Right on 1A Avenue, then continue right on 65B Street, opposite the school.

9.8   Left on 3rd Avenue, which becomes Boundary Bay Road.

12.3   Keep right on Beach Grove Road.

13.4   Right on the footpath to the dyke and retrace your outward route.

17.6   South foot of 72nd Street.

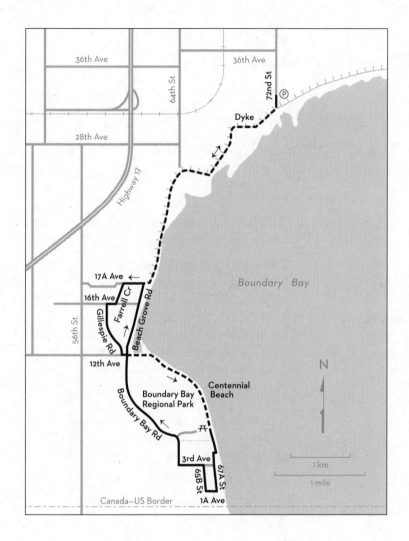

> 17 MUD BAY

Surrey

· · · · ·

ROUND TRIP	14.3 km (9 miles)
TERRAIN	Gravel paths and dyke, paved roads; flat
TRAFFIC VOLUME	Very low
ALLOW	1 ½ to 2 ½ hours
HIGHLIGHTS	Shoreline views, waterfowl, shorebirds, raptors, Delta Heritage Airpark
PICNIC SPOT	Delta Heritage Airpark at 7.1 km
STARTING POINT	Mud Bay Park
HOW TO GET THERE	Mud Bay Park can only be reached from Colebrook Road. Leave Hwy 99 at exit 20 and drive east on Ladner Trunk Road (Hwy 10). After crossing Annacis Highway (Hwy 91) turn right on 120th Street. Turn left on New McLellan Road and right on 125A Street. Bear left onto Station Road, left on Colebrook Road, then right, across the railway tracks, on 127A Street. Follow the park access road left to its end at the gravel parking lot.
	BY TRANSIT: There is no convenient transit option at this time.
WHEN TO GO	May and June to see wildflowers along the dyke.
CONNECTS WITH	Boundary Bay, page 74

IN SPITE of its uninviting name and circuitous approach, Surrey's Mud Bay Park is popular with walkers, joggers and cyclists. Certainly it is a safe ride for rusty cyclists and families with young

On Delta South Surrey Greenway

children; more ambitious riders can pedal the entire 16-kilometre dyke to Boundary Bay.

Two loop trails around the shoreline afford views of the tussocks and tidal channels of the shallow bay. Sandpipers probe the mudflats or soar and wheel above the water to confound a raiding falcon; with binoculars you might spot harbour seals hauled out on the sandbars where the Serpentine and Nicomekl Rivers empty into the eastern end of the bay. Note, though, that the shoreline trails are closed to cyclists from October 15 to April 15 to provide a quiet haven for over-wintering and migratory birds.

A further attraction to this trip around Mud Bay is the suggested picnic spot and turnaround point at Delta Heritage Airpark, home of the Boundary Bay Flying Club, and now part of Boundary Bay Regional Park. Here you can watch light planes take off or land while you eat your lunch. A coffee shop, run by volunteers, is usually open weekends; if there is no one around to serve you, you are welcome to fix yourself a coffee and leave your money on the counter. On the second Sunday of the month, the club hosts an egg and pancake breakfast.

For your return to Mud Bay Park, our route makes a foray into the farmland between the highway and the bay—a short loop on quiet roads before rejoining the dyke.

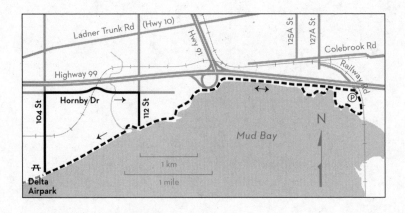

KM THE ROUTE

0.0 Mud Bay Park. Begin the loop trail from the southeast corner of the parking lot. Stay right along the shoreline.

1.2 Left on the main path.

1.4 Left on the second shoreline loop trail. Look for the giant cedar driftwood log on the left.

1.9 Left on the main path. After about 2 km, the path veers away from the highway and becomes the Delta South Surrey Greenway.

5.2 Foot of 112th Street. Continue on the dyke.

7.1 Foot of 104th Street. Delta Heritage Airpark. Picnic tables, coffee shop, toilet.

7.1 To return partway by paved roads, go north on 104th Street.

8.5 Right on Hornby Drive.

10.2 Right on 112th Street.

10.8 Left onto the dyke.

14.3 Mud Bay Park parking lot.

> 18 SEMIAHMOO PENINSULA

South Surrey

· · · · ·

ROUND TRIP	18.3 km (11 ½ miles)
TERRAIN	Paved roads and unpaved trail; a few hills
TRAFFIC VOLUME	Low, except heavy at times on Crescent Road and around 152nd Street
ALLOW	2 to 3 hours
HIGHLIGHTS	Semiahmoo Trail, Nicomekl River, Elgin Heritage Park and tidal flats, Stewart Farmhouse, Crescent Park
PICNIC SPOT	Crescent Park at 10.7 km
STARTING POINT	Bakerview Park parking lot on 154th Street
HOW TO GET THERE	BY CAR: From King George Boulevard (Hwy 99A) in South Surrey, turn west on 20th Avenue, then left (south) on 154th Street. The park is on the corner of 154th Street and 18th Avenue.
	BY TRANSIT: Take the bus to 152 Street at 20th Avenue and ride to the starting point.
WHEN TO GO	See wildflowers along the trail in July; Stewart Farmhouse has events throughout the year, e.g. Victoria Day Open House in May, a pioneer fair in July, Apple Days in September.

ONCE INHABITED by Coast Salish people, this sunny corner of Surrey is now a suburban retreat, well served by parks and beaches. Some reminders of its Aboriginal and pioneer history have been preserved, however. You'll cycle a remnant of the Semiahmoo Trail, an early Native trail that linked tribal villages to the Fraser River fishing grounds and that later became a road for transporting goods and mail between New Westminster and what is now Blaine, Washington. The remaining fragment is preserved and maintained by community members, the Friends of Semiahmoo Heritage Trail.

You'll continue cycling off-road as you follow the Nicomekl Greenway to Elgin Heritage Park, home of the Stewart Farmhouse, built in 1894. The Stewart family dyked and farmed the land beside the Nicomekl River and helped to establish the Elgin school and community hall. Their home is now restored as a living museum, where pioneer skills are demonstrated. Your route includes a side trip around tidal flats—a haven for songbirds, waterfowl and shorebirds, complete with an owl barn. At low tide you may see sandpipers and Long-billed Dowitchers probing the mud for worms.

After tackling the hill on Crescent Road, you can take a break in Crescent Park amid beautiful second-growth forest before completing the circuit via a neighbourhood path and quiet residential streets.

KM **THE ROUTE**

0.0 Bakerview Park parking lot.

Left on 154th Street.

0.4 Left on 20th Avenue. Cross 152nd Street at the traffic lights.

0.9 Right on 151A Avenue.

1.0 Straight ahead on Semiahmoo Trail. Please cycle slowly on this narrow, winding trail and give way to pedestrians. Cross 23A Avenue.

1.7 Cross 24th Avenue. Descend through the forest.

2.6 An information kiosk tells the history of Semiahmoo Trail. Go right onto the overpass and right at the end of it.

Cross 28th Avenue at the traffic light.

2.8 Go straight ahead onto a paved section of Semiahmoo Trail.

On the Nicomekl dyke path

3.5 Pass Semiahmoo Park on your left. A path on your right leads to benches overlooking a pond before rejoining Semiahmoo Trail.

3.7 Cross 32nd Avenue, then 34th Avenue.

4.5 Elgin Heritage School. Note: Until a better provision is made for cyclists to turn left on Crescent Road, we recommend crossing 144th Street opposite the school and walking your bike left along the sidewalk on Crescent Road for about 50 m, until you have a clearer view of oncoming traffic before crossing.

4.8 Go right on the shortcut before the Esso station, pass the roundabout and cross Elgin Road before reaching the "No Entry" signs.

4.9 Cairn commemorating the Semiahmoo Trail. Go left between the posts onto the Nicomekl Greenway. Follow the path around Nico Wynd Golf Course.

6.3 Right at the information board before entering Nico Wynd works yard. Follow this path past an old house and alongside Crescent Road to enter Elgin Heritage Park.

7.0 Left to the Stewart Farmhouse. Apple orchard, pole barn, toilets. From the farmhouse, turn right, then left through the lower parking lot to continue on the trail.

7.5 Elgin tidal flats. Go right at the fork before entering the parking lot. Stay on the perimeter trail around the flats. Shorebirds, raptors, views of Nicomekl River.

8.6 Right through the gates and right on Crescent Road. Hills.

9.7 Left on 132nd Street.

10.1 Right on 28th Avenue.

10.7 Left through the parking lot into Crescent Park. Picnic tables, benches along the way, toilets. From the park entrance, take the trail that passes behind the washroom building. Stay on the main trail, passing a playground on your left.

10.9 Right at the T-junction after the playground.

Pass a pond on your left—a good place to spot frogs and turtles. Continue on the main trail.

11.1 Left at the 4-way trail junction with a tree in the middle. Pass sports fields on your left.

11.7 Right onto 132nd Street at the gate. Cross 24th Avenue.

11.9 At the intersection with 23A Avenue, take the neighbourhood trail on the left, passing between houses.

12.2 Straight ahead where a paved path intersects.

12.4 Right on 132A Street. Cross 20th Avenue.

13.0 Left on 18A Avenue. Cross 134th Street onto 19th Avenue.

13.7 Right on 136th Street.

13.9 Left on 18th Avenue. Cross 140th Street.

15.1 Left on 142nd Street.

15.3 Right on 18A Avenue. Cross 144th Street onto 18th Avenue.

16.2 Right on 146th Street.

16.4 Left on 17th Avenue. Cross 148th Street at the stop sign.

17.0 Right on Southmere Crescent.

17.3 Left on Martin Drive at the traffic light. Cross 152nd Street onto 18th Avenue.

18.1 Left on 154th Street.

18.3 Left into Bakerview Park parking lot.

> 19   PITT POLDER

Pitt Meadows/
Fraser Valley Regional District

. . . . .

ROUND TRIP	27.1 km (17 miles)
TERRAIN	Paved roads and gravel dyke; flat
TRAFFIC VOLUME	Low
ALLOW	2 ½ to 3 ½ hours
HIGHLIGHTS	Pitt Polder, Pitt Lake, mountain views, osprey nests, Alouette River
PICNIC SPOT	Grant Narrows Regional Park at 13.6 km
STARTING POINT	Menzies Crossing parking area on Harris Road, south of Alouette River bridge
HOW TO GET THERE	BY CAR: From Lougheed Highway (Hwy 7), turn left on Dewdney Trunk Road just east of Pitt River Bridge. Turn left again on Harris Road and drive 2 km to Alouette River bridge.
	BY TRANSIT: Catch the West Coast Express to Pitt Meadows Station or take the bus to Harris Road at Dewdney Trunk Road and ride to the starting point.
WHEN TO GO	Watch for young osprey on the nests in May and June; buy local blueberries in August.
CONNECTS WITH	Pitt River Regional Greenway, page 90; Alouette River, page 94

Grant Narrows Regional Park

NATURE TAMED and untamed could be the theme for this ride. First, the polder: land wrested from the flood plain by human ingenuity. As early as 1911, attempts were made to dyke the area, all ending in flooding or financial disaster. It took Dutch immigrant engineers (and Dutch investment) to overcome the problems. During the 1950s, the first farmsteads were laid out, each with a silo, barn and milking parlour and tenanted by a Dutch farmer.

The marshy northern half of the polder is designated as a Wildlife Management Area and extends to Pitt Lake. From the shores of the 26-kilometre-long lake, the Coast Mountains rise dramatically, often bearing weighty clouds on their shoulders. To the north, from its headwaters on a snowy peak in Garibaldi Park, the upper Pitt River flows through the lake and out again through Grant Narrows, fighting the tides on its way to join the Fraser River.

It is worth cycling out along the Pitt Lake dyke for a view of the lake and marsh. Keep a look out for ospreys—their nests have been built on top of the pilings at the edge of the foreshore.

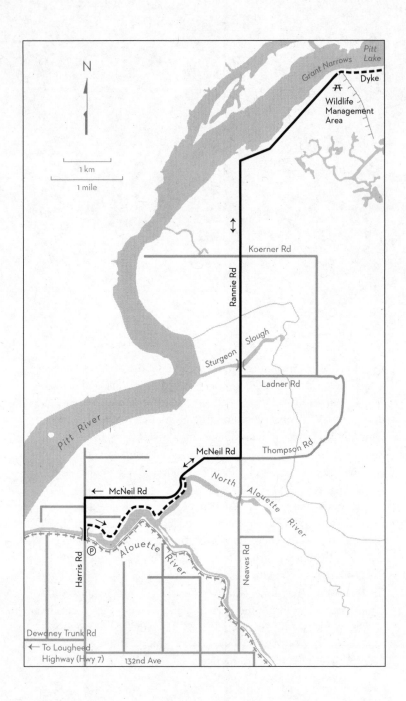

N

1 km
1 mile

Grant Narrows   Pitt Lake

Dyke

Wildlife
Management
Area

Koerner Rd

Rannie Rd

Sturgeon   Slough

Ladner Rd

Thompson Rd

Pitt River

McNeil Rd

North   Alouette   River

McNeil Rd

Harris Rd   Ⓟ

Alouette   River

Neaves Rd

Dewdney Trunk Rd

← To Lougheed
Highway (Hwy 7)   132nd Ave

0.0 Menzies Crossing parking area. Right (north) on Harris Road and over the bridge.

0.2 Right onto the dyke path on the north side of Alouette River.

3.2 Leave the dyke and continue to the right on McNeil Road. Blueberry farms and tree nurseries.

4.7 Left on Rannie Road.

6.5 Cross the bridge over Sturgeon Slough.

13.6 Grant Narrows Regional Park at Pitt Lake. Picnic tables, toilets, concession, canoe rental, walking trails.

OPTION: Cycle Pitt Lake dyke for wider views. The inner dykes are for walkers only.

13.6 Retrace your outward route on Rannie Road.

22.5 Right on McNeil Road.

26.3 Left on Harris Road.

27.1 Left into Menzies Crossing parking area.

> 20 PITT RIVER REGIONAL GREENWAY

Pitt Meadows

. . . . .

ROUND TRIP	28.1 km (17 ½ miles)
TERRAIN	Paved roads and gravel dyke
TRAFFIC VOLUME	Low
ALLOW	2 ½ to 3 ½ hours
HIGHLIGHTS	Fraser, Pitt and Alouette Rivers; mountain views; light airplane activity at Pitt Meadows Airport; berry fields; ospreys; songbirds
PICNIC SPOT	A bench on the Pitt or Alouette River dyke after 10.3 km, or picnic tables at Menzies Crossing (Alouette River bridge on Harris Road) at 14 km.
STARTING POINT	Harris Landing at the south foot of Harris Road
HOW TO GET THERE	BY CAR: From Lougheed Highway (Hwy 7) east of the Pitt River Bridge, turn south on Harris Road and drive to its end at the dyke. BY TRANSIT: Catch the West Coast Express to Pitt Meadows Station or take the bus to Harris Road at Hammond Road and ride to the starting point.
WHEN TO GO	Summer to hear songbirds along the dyke; October to see crimson-coloured blueberry bushes.
CONNECTS WITH	Pitt Polder, page 86; Alouette River, page 94

Fraser River viewpoint

I'T'S HARD to beat this traffic-free jaunt along the Pitt River Regional Greenway for scenery and interest. Simply settle into a comfortable cruising speed and let the sights unfold before your eyes:
rivers and mountains, boats and airplanes, farms and cows, berry
fields and birds.

Metro Vancouver is working with municipalities and community groups to create a network of greenways throughout the
region. The Pitt River Greenway uses the existing dykes, upgraded
for bicycles, with added access points, links with municipal trails
and an underpass beneath the Pitt River Bridge. The greenway may
eventually continue for 30 kilometres to Grant Narrows Regional
Park at Pitt Lake.

Note: At the time of writing, construction is still going on
around the Pitt River Bridge. The underpass is in place and being
used by eager cyclists, but until the work is finished users should
obey any temporary signs and detours.

0.0 Harris Landing parking area. Information kiosk, toilets, view of the Fraser River and Barnston Island from an interpretive trail for walkers. Cycle west on the dyke path.

1.0 Foot of Baynes Road. A short path to the left leads to a viewpoint.

1.7 Pitt Meadows Airport. The trail passes through a tunnel.

3.4 Continue on the paved road beyond the gate. A sawmill is on your left. The gravel dyke path resumes from the end of 176th Street.

5.2 Confluence of the Pitt and Fraser Rivers. Cranberry fields inland.

9.3 Kennedy Road parking area. Continue on the dyke path. Pitt River Bridge is ahead.

9.6 Enter the railway underpass. Blind corner. Continue on the paved underpass beneath the Pitt River Bridge.

10.3 Left through the gate onto the dyke path. View upstream toward Burke Ridge and the mountains around Pitt Lake. Blueberry fields inland.

12.6 Confluence of the Alouette and Pitt Rivers. Pitt Meadows Marina. Watch for ospreys. Continue eastward on the Alouette River dyke.

14.0 Menzies Crossing. Cross Harris Road to the parking and picnic area. Riverside picnic tables, toilets, Trans Canada Trail pavilion.

14.0 Retrace your outward route along the dykes and through the bridge and railway underpasses.

18.8 Kennedy Road parking area. If you don't wish to retrace your outward route along the dyke, lift your bicycle over the gate (if necessary) and go right on Kennedy Road.

19.8 Kennedy becomes Woolridge Road.

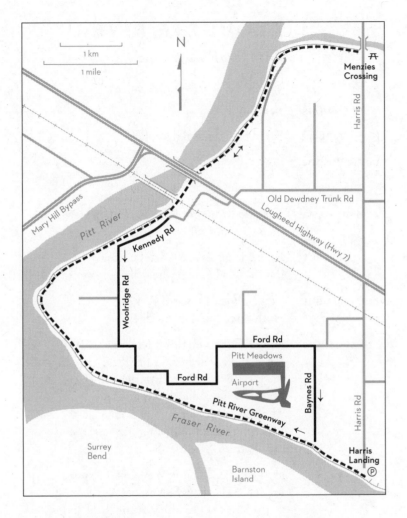

21.3 Left at the T-junction onto Ford Road. Follow Ford Road through several changes of direction. Watch for skydivers over Pitt Meadows Airport.

25.5 Right on Baynes Road.

27.1 Left onto the dyke path.

28.1 Harris Landing parking area.

> 21 ALOUETTE RIVER

Pitt Meadows/Maple Ridge

. . . . .

ROUND TRIP	20.9 km (13 miles)
TERRAIN	Paved roads, gravel dyke; flat
TRAFFIC VOLUME	Low
ALLOW	2 to 3 hours
HIGHLIGHTS	Alouette River, Pitt River, mountain views, herons, waterfowl
PICNIC SPOT	Riverside tables at Menzies Crossing (Harris Road parking area) at 6.4 km or 12 km
STARTING POINT	Jerry Sulina Municipal Park on 210th Street in Maple Ridge
HOW TO GET THERE	BY CAR: From Lougheed Highway (Hwy 7), turn left on Dewdney Trunk Road just east of the Pitt River Bridge. Turn right on Harris Road and immediately left on Dewdney Trunk, which later becomes 132nd Avenue. Jerry Sulina Park is on the left, just after the bend onto 210th Street. BY TRANSIT: Catch the West Coast Express to Maple Meadows Station or take the bus to 203rd Street at Dewdney Trunk Road and ride to the starting point.
WHEN TO GO	August to buy local blueberries.
CONNECTS WITH	Pitt Polder, page 86; Pitt River Regional Greenway, page 90

Alouette River

THE ALOUETTE River (usually referred to as the South Alouette) rises on Mount Robie Reid, flows into Alouette Lake and spills out through the dam at the reservoir's south end to be joined in due course by the smaller North Alouette River. Together they join the Pitt River on its way to empty into the Fraser. The dykes of these three rivers encompass and protect the low-lying land of Pitt Meadows. Here, as in other parts of the Fraser Valley, many dyke paths are designated and maintained as regional greenways, providing a network of trails for outdoors lovers.

On this easy family ride, you have a grandstand view of the fields and waterways with their backdrop of mountains. These dykes are popular with cyclists, walkers and joggers, but there is room for everyone and most are good about sharing the trail. *Alouette* is the French word for skylark; you might not spot a lark as you ride along, but you're sure to see herons fishing around the riverbanks and ducks dabbling in the backwaters.

An added jaunt to the mouth of the Alouette and along Chatham Reach—named for William Pitt, Earl of Chatham— offers superb views toward Pitt Lake and opposite to Addington Marsh and the knolls of Minnekhada Regional Park.

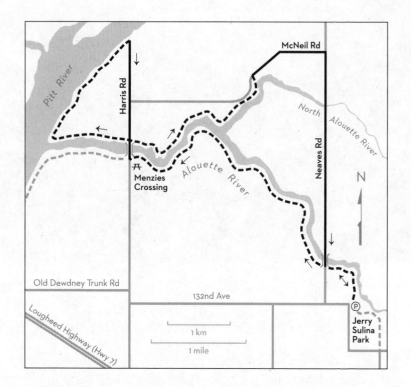

KM **THE ROUTE**

0.0 Jerry Sulina Municipal Park. Climb the path from the parking lot onto the dyke and head left along the dyke path.

1.2 Cross Neaves Road and continue along the dyke.

4.4 The confluence of the Alouette and North Alouette Rivers.

6.4 Menzies Crossing. Parking lot and picnic area beside Alouette River bridge. Trans Canada Trail Pavilion, toilets. To continue, cross the bridge to the north bank of the river and cycle westward (downstream) on the dyke path.

7.9 There are boathouses and pleasure boats as you approach the river mouth. Continue northward beside the Pitt River (Chatham Reach). Views of mountains, shoreline marshes and river traffic.

10.2 The north end of Harris Road meets the dyke.

OPTION: You could continue on the dyke path for another kilometre to a gate barring access to Sheridan Hill quarry, where you must turn around. Otherwise, leave the dyke here and cycle south on Harris Road.

12.0 Left (upstream) on the north bank of the Alouette immediately before the bridge and Menzies Crossing parking area.

15.0 Leave the dyke at the exit onto McNeil Road and continue right on McNeil. Blueberry fields and tree nurseries.

16.4 Right on Neaves Road.

17.3 Cross the bridge over the North Alouette and continue on Neaves.

19.7 After crossing the bridge over the South Alouette, turn left onto the dyke path.

20.9 Jerry Sulina Municipal Park parking lot.

> 22 GOLDEN EARS PARK

Maple Ridge

. . . . .

ROUND TRIP	24 km (15 miles) or 36 km (22 ½ miles)
TERRAIN	Paved road, some unpaved road and optional trail; gentle undulations
TRAFFIC VOLUME	Low, except moderate on Fern Crescent
ALLOW	2 to 3 hours, or up to 4 hours for Gold Creek option
HIGHLIGHTS	Alouette Lake and beach, coastal forest, views of mountain peaks, Gold Creek (optional), Maple Ridge Park
PICNIC SPOT	Alouette Lake day-use area at 12 km
STARTING POINT	Maple Ridge Park on 232nd Street
HOW TO GET THERE	BY CAR: From the Lougheed Highway (Hwy 7) in Maple Ridge, follow Golden Ears Park signs north as far as Maple Ridge Park on the corner of 232nd Street and Fern Crescent.
	BY TRANSIT: Catch the West Coast Express to Port Haney Station or take the bus to 232nd Street at 128th Avenue and ride to the starting point.
WHEN TO GO	Swim at Alouette Lake in July or August.

EW ROUTE instructions are needed on this uncomplicated ride into Golden Ears Provincial Park. On Fern Crescent, you follow the winding course of the Alouette River, entering the southern end of the park beneath the impassive gaze of a carved wooden mountain goat. Thereafter, you'll notice hiking and equestrian trails leading into the forest on either side of the road.

Second-growth forest

Many will be content to end the ride with a lazy picnic and swim at Alouette Lake. More energetic cyclists can continue to Gold Creek, where you can follow a short trail to North Beach or take a 2.7-kilometre walk along the creek to Lower Falls. Cycling is not allowed on Lower Falls Trail, so pack your bike lock if you intend to include this scenic walk in your itinerary.

Beyond a rugged mountain barrier at its northern end, Golden Ears Park abuts the even larger Garibaldi Provincial Park, making a vast, unbroken stretch of wilderness parkland. The Alouette Valley through which you ride was once the site of B.C.'s largest railway-logging operation. During the 1920s, giant firs and cedars fell to the axe and saw—a decade-long harvest that ended when fire swept through the valley in 1931. Cycling between the ranks of today's second-growth forest, you catch glimpses of the ramparts to the west: Alouette Mountain, Evans Peak and the twin peaks of Mount Blanshard known as the Golden Ears.

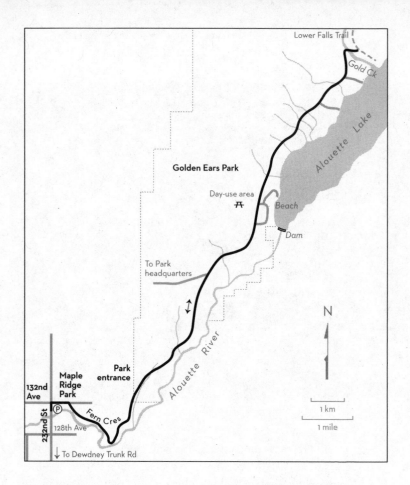

KM	THE ROUTE

0.0 Maple Ridge Park parking lot. Go east on 132nd Avenue then bear right onto Fern Crescent. This narrow, winding road may be busy at weekends.

4.1 Park entrance. Wooden mountain goat.

12.0 Right to Alouette Lake day-use area. Swimming, long sandy beach, picnic tables, toilets.

OPTION: Continue on park road for 6 km to Gold Creek day-use area. One-km cycling/hiking trail to North Beach; 2.7-km walking trail to Lower Falls. Otherwise,

12.0 Retrace your outward route to Maple Ridge Park.

24.0 Maple Ridge Park parking lot.

> 23 WHONNOCK LAKE

Maple Ridge

. . . . .

ROUND TRIP	23.5 km (14 ¾ miles)
TERRAIN	Paved roads and unpaved trail (walk only); several hills, some steep
TRAFFIC VOLUME	Low, except on Jackson Road
ALLOW	2 ½ to 3 ½ hours
HIGHLIGHTS	Quiet, winding roads, woodland trail, side trip to Bell-Irving Fish Hatchery, Kanaka Creek, Whonnock Lake
PICNIC SPOT	Whonnock Lake at 11.5 km
STARTING POINT	Albion Park on 104th Avenue
HOW TO GET THERE	BY CAR: From Lougheed Highway (Hwy 7) east of Haney, turn north on 240th Street, then right on 104th Avenue. The park is on the right after 0.8 km.
	BY TRANSIT: Take the bus to 104th Avenue at Jackson Road.
WHEN TO GO	Swim at Whonnock Lake in July and August.

O N A day when you're feeling energetic and a bit adventurous, you'll enjoy this sporting little ride among the winding lanes near Kanaka Creek.

Maple Ridge abounds in roads that almost but not quite connect with each other, so your route has many turnings before it reaches Whonnock Lake. To circumvent one of these gaps in the road system, we've directed you along a foot trail through the woods for a short distance. This is primarily a hiking and equestrian trail;

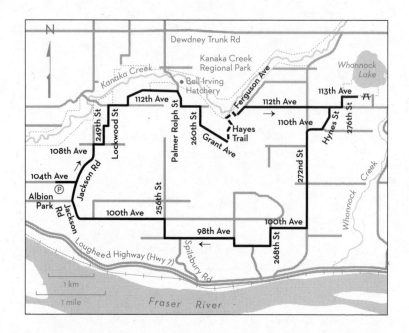

please walk your bike where necessary and be prepared to take a small stream in your stride. This digression is far more pleasant than the alternative, which is to cycle 4 kilometres along the Dewdney Trunk Road amid speeding traffic.

A side trip to the Bell-Irving Fish Hatchery on Kanaka Creek is worthwhile. Free tours, on which you may see juvenile salmon and trout in the troughs and rearing ponds, are offered most days. The hatchery releases large numbers of salmon fry into the creek each spring.

After a rest, and perhaps a swim, at Whonnock Lake, you can look forward to plenty of freewheeling on the homeward lap.

KM THE ROUTE

0.0 Albion Park parking lot. East on 104th Avenue.

0.5 Left on Jackson Road, which becomes 248th Street.

1.5 Right on 108th Avenue.

1.7 Left on 249th Street, which becomes Lockwood Street.

2.6 Right on 112th Avenue.

3.1 Left on 252nd Street, which becomes 112th Avenue.

4.4 OPTION: For the side trip to Bell-Irving hatchery, turn left on 256th Street, then right to the hatchery after 0.2 km. Otherwise,

4.4 Right on Palmer Rolph Street.

Left on 112th Avenue.

5.2 Right on 260th Street (signed "No Thru Rd"), which becomes Grant Avenue.

6.3 End of Grant Avenue. Go straight ahead on the signposted Hayes Trail. Please walk bikes on this trail.

Go left at the first trail junction. Cross the bridge over the creek and keep left. Cross the second creek—there may be a plank bridge.

7.8 Right onto a wide equestrian trail that emerges on Ferguson Avenue.

8.1 Right on 112th Avenue.

10.4 Left on 276th Street at the sign to Whonnock Lake, and follow the road to the main parking lot near the beach.

11.5 Beach parking. Picnic tables, toilets, swimming.

11.5 Retrace your route to 112th Avenue.

12.6 Right on 112th Avenue.

12.8 Left on Hynes Street.

13.3 Right on 110th Avenue.

13.6 Left on 272nd Street. Narrow shoulder—use caution.

15.8 Right on 100th Avenue. Sudden steep hill—find a low gear quickly!

16.6 Left on 268th Street. Steep downhill.

Right on 98th Avenue.

17.8 Jog right on 264th Street.

18.0 Left on 98th Avenue.

19.6 Right on 256th Street.

20.0 Left on 100th Avenue, which becomes Jackson Road.

22.4 Bear right on Jackson Road where 102nd Avenue branches left.

22.8 Left on 104th Avenue.

23.3 Albion Park parking lot.

Rearing ponds, Bell-Irving hatchery

Canada goose

> 24 STAVE DAMS

Mission

. . . . .

ROUND TRIP	26 km (16 ¼ miles)
TERRAIN	Paved roads; rolling hills, some steep
TRAFFIC VOLUME	Low to moderate
ALLOW	2 ½ to 4 hours
HIGHLIGHTS	Stave and Ruskin Dams, Stave Falls Powerhouse, Hayward Lake, Railway Trail (optional), side trip to Rolley Lake Provincial Park, Stave River
PICNIC SPOT	Mill Pond on Dewdney Trunk Road at 10.8 km or Hayward Lake Recreation Area at 18.6 km
STARTING POINT	Ruskin Recreation Site on Hayward Street east of Ruskin Dam
HOW TO GET THERE	BY CAR: Follow Lougheed Highway (Hwy 7) east from Maple Ridge toward Mission and turn left on 287th Street. After about 3 km turn right to cross Ruskin Dam and continue for less than 1 km to signposted Ruskin Recreation Site.
	BY TRANSIT: Take the bus to Lougheed Highway (Hwy 7) at 280th Street and ride to the starting point.
WHEN TO GO	See the dams at their best in July and August.

ALTHOUGH FAIRLY challenging, this circuit around the Stave Dams near Mission is not beyond the ability of any cyclist equipped with low gears, good brakes and a bit of courage. The landscape is majestic, whether viewed from the dam walls or from the rolling hills of historic Dewdney Trunk Road—originally an overland coach route from Dewdney to Port Moody.

The generation of hydroelectric power from Alouette and Stave Lakes began in the early 1900s. Before the construction of the Stave and Ruskin Dams, the Stave River flowed unchecked through a forested valley. Today, it passes through the Stave Falls powerhouse into Hayward Lake Reservoir before being released from the Ruskin powerhouse to flow into the Fraser River.

Optional side trips to Rolley Lake Provincial Park and Hayward Lake Recreation Site reward the energetic. From the latter, cyclists with a liking for off-road riding can follow the 6-kilometre Railway Trail to the Ruskin Dam.

Note: Ruskin Dam is scheduled for seismic upgrading during which the Ruskin Dam Bridge and Recreation Site may be closed at times. Before setting out on this ride, phone BC Hydro Community Relations at 1-800-663-1377.

KM THE ROUTE

0.0 Ruskin Recreation Site. Right (east) onto Hayward Street.

1.1 Left on Keystone Avenue. A steep uphill for 1.2 km, then a more gradual ascent.

7.4 Left on Dewdney Trunk Road. Uphill again.

10.8 Mill Pond is on your right. This could be a well-deserved rest or picnic spot. There are no facilities.

10.8 Continue on Dewdney Trunk Road. You follow gentle rolling hills through Steelhead, then make a steep, winding descent to the Stave Dams.

17.8 Cross Stave Falls Dams. Watch for oncoming traffic and beware of the railway track in the roadbed.

OPTION: Follow the signs to visit the Stave Falls Powerhouse and Visitor Centre. Self-guided tours, history and hydroelectric operation, theatre, gift shop.

18.6 OPTION: Left goes to Hayward Lake Recreation Area. Picnic tables, toilets, beach, Railway Trail to Ruskin Dam. Otherwise continue west on Dewdney Trunk Road.

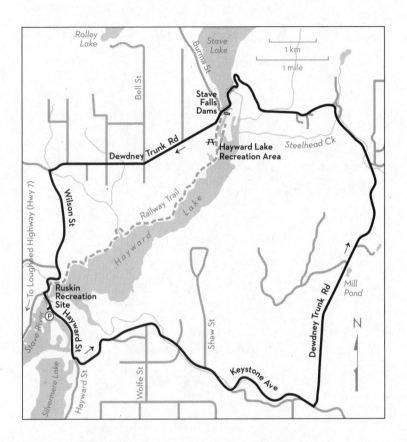

20.9 OPTION: Right on Bell Street leads to Rolley Lake Provincial Park. Picnic area, beach, trails, interpretive centre. Add 7 km for this side trip. Otherwise continue west on Dewdney Trunk Road.

22.5 Left on Wilson Street. Steep winding descent.

25.5 Left across Ruskin Dam.

26.0 Right to Ruskin Recreation Site. Picnic tables, toilets, path to spawning channels and Stave River.

BARNSTON ISLAND

Langley

· · · · ·

ROUND TRIP	10 km (6 ¼ miles) or more
TERRAIN	Paved road; flat
TRAFFIC VOLUME	Very low
ALLOW	1 to 1 ½ hours
HIGHLIGHTS	Ferry crossing, farms, river and mountain views, Robert Point Regional Park
PICNIC SPOT	Robert Point at 8.9 km
STARTING POINT	Ferry slip at the end of 104th Avenue (Hjorth Road)
HOW TO GET THERE	BY CAR: Leave Hwy 1, east of the Port Mann Bridge, at exit 50 and drive north on 160th Street. Turn right on 104th Avenue and drive for about 3.5 km to the parking lot at the ferry slip.
	BY TRANSIT: Take the bus to 104th Avenue at 168th Street and ride to the starting point.
WHEN TO GO	Look for wild roses in bloom in June.

SOMETIMES YOU want a safe, undemanding ride that even little legs and wheels can manage. Barnston Island, lying in the Fraser River opposite Surrey Bend, is a favourite with cycling families. Leave your car at the slip; a free ferry ride—sound your horn to summon the boat—is part of the fun.

The paved road you cycle on is the top of a dyke encircling the entire island. Inland, the landscape is a patchwork of fields, while the river beyond the dyke provides a changing scene. In Parsons Channel, fishboats, barges and float planes go about their business

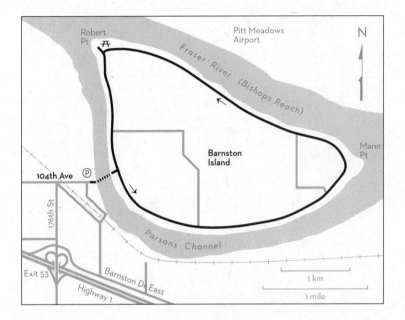

to the music of a nearby sawmill. After rounding Mann Point at the island's eastern end, you enter Bishops Reach. Paths lead down to the river, where you can look across the log booms to Pitt Meadows Airport on the opposite shore and upstream to Golden Ears Bridge.

All too soon, you reach Robert Point at the northwest tip of the island. Follow the loop trail to the beach and picnic site. A short homestretch, enhanced by a view of Mount Baker, brings you back to the ferry stage. Not long enough? Go round again.

KM   **THE ROUTE**

0.0   Disembark from the ferry and go right to begin a counterclockwise circuit. River traffic in Parsons Channel.

4.3   Mann Point. Wild roses in summer. View upstream to Golden Ears.

8.9   Robert Point Regional Park with picnic tables, toilets. View downstream toward the Port Mann Bridge.

10.0   Ferry slip.

> 26 FORT-TO-FORT TRAIL

Langley

. . . . .

ROUND TRIP	25.6 km (16 miles)
TERRAIN	Paved roads and unpaved trail; rolling hills
TRAFFIC VOLUME	Low to moderate
ALLOW	2 ½ to 3 ½ hours
HIGHLIGHTS	Telegraph Trail, Fort Langley, Fraser River views, historic site, Fort-to-Fort Trail, Edgewater Bar
PICNIC SPOT	Fort Langley National Historic Site picnic area at 12.5 km
STARTING POINT	West Langley Park on 208th Street in Walnut Grove
HOW TO GET THERE	BY CAR: Leave Hwy 1 at exit 58 and drive north on 200th Street. Turn right on 88th Avenue East then left on 208th Street. The park is on the right a few metres beyond the 93rd Avenue intersection.
	BY TRANSIT: Take the bus to 96th Avenue and 208th Street.
WHEN TO GO	Attend Fort Langley's May Day Parade or Brigade Days in August.
CONNECTS WITH	Glen Valley, page 114

LEAVING WALNUT GROVE, you speed down a long and glorious descent on Telegraph Trail. Thereafter, there is much to stop and look at on this historical ride.

Entering Fort Langley from its back door on River Road, you glimpse the restored Hudson's Bay fort from below its stockade.

Site of the first Fort Langley

Built on this site in 1839 as a fur-trading post, Fort Langley became a large and busy centre, employing an army of craftsmen to serve trappers, farmers and gold miners. Today, within the log palisade, the fort comprises both reconstructed and original buildings, including the Big House (the officers' quarters), the general store, a cooperage and a blacksmith's forge. Costumed staff members are on hand to answer any questions.

Four kilometres downstream, along your route, is the site of the first Fort Langley, hurriedly built in 1827 as a base for the Hudson's Bay Company's growing trade with the Native peoples of the Fraser River. A hiking/cycling route, the Fort-to-Fort Trail, links the two sites. Opposite the commemorative cairn is a restored 1909 homestead, as well as access to the Houston Trail (for walkers and horseback riders only) through the forest—all part of Derby Reach Regional Park.

Finally, via Edge Farm Trail, you arrive at the riverfront camping and picnic area at Edgewater Bar before heading home.

0.0 West Langley Park parking lot. Take the paved path to the right of the sports field, keeping right past the playground onto 93rd Avenue.

0.2 Left on 93rd Avenue.

0.7 Right on 212th Street.

1.3 Right on Walnut Grove Drive. Cross 88th Avenue.

2.6 Left on 85th Avenue at the T-junction.

3.1 Right on Telegraph Trail.

Cross 216th Street and begin a long downhill with views.

6.2 Left on Glover Road. Use caution at this junction.

6.7 Right on Rawlison Crescent.

7.5 Stay left on Rawlison where 232nd Street joins. Use extreme caution at this turning.

8.5 Railway tunnel. Go uphill shortly after. Mountain Conservation Centre is on your right.

9.3 Keep left at junction onto 240th Street (may not be signposted at this point).

10.6 Left on River Road.

12.3 Left on Mavis Avenue.

12.5 Fort Langley National Historic Site. Museums, picnic tables, toilets.

12.8 From Mavis Avenue, turn right on Glover Road and cross the railway tracks. The signposted Fort-to-Fort Trail begins just past the Fort Pub opposite.

13.0 Left onto the Fort-to-Fort Trail. The wide gravel path beside the Bedford Channel of the Fraser River skirts a residential area; opposite is Brae Island.

14.3 Salmon River Pump Station. Viewing platform. The trail narrows, with ups and downs. Please give way to walkers.

15.4 Right on Allard Crescent. Roadside trail.

16.1 Right on Fort-to-Fort Trail along Derby Bluffs.

17.1 Derby Reach Regional Park Heritage Area. A cairn marks the site of the original fort. Houston House (not open to the public) and

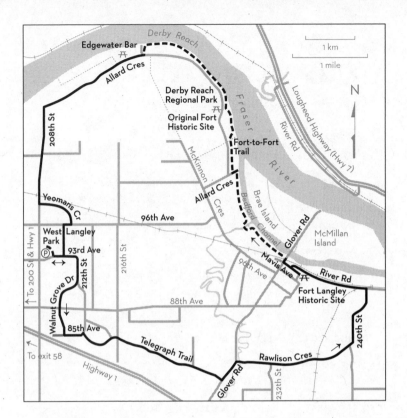

restored farm buildings opposite. Picnic tables, toilets.

Continue on the gravel trail (Edge Farm Trail) descending from the cairn. Views across the river to Kanaka Creek Riverfront Park.

18.7 Keep straight ahead on the gravel road past the campsites.

19.4 Edgewater Bar. Picnic tables, toilets, camping, fishing.

19.5 Right on Allard Crescent past fields dyked for cranberry bogs.

21.8 Left on 208th Street.

23.7 Left on Yeomans Crescent.

24.5 Right on 96th Avenue, then immediately left on 210th Street.

25.2 Right on 93rd Avenue.

25.4 Right onto the path at the playground.

25.6 West Langley Park parking lot.

> 27 GLEN VALLEY

Langley/Abbotsford

. . . . .

ROUND TRIP	34.9 km (21 ¾ miles) or 37.9 km (23 ¾ miles)
TERRAIN	Paved roads, optional unpaved dyke path; some flat, some hills; several railway crossings
TRAFFIC VOLUME	Low, except moderate on River Road
ALLOW	3 ½ to 4 ½ hours
HIGHLIGHTS	Fort Langley village and museums, Telegraph Trail, Fraser River, Glen Valley Regional Park, Fort Winery
PICNIC SPOT	Poplar Bar at 22.8 km
STARTING POINT	Fort Langley National Historic Park, Mavis Avenue at River Road
HOW TO GET THERE	BY CAR: Leave Hwy 1 at exit 58 or 66, following signs to Fort Langley. From Glover Road, turn right onto Mavis Avenue and then left into the Fort Langley Historic Site parking lot.
	BY TRANSIT: Take the bus to Glover Road at 96th Avenue and ride to the starting point.
WHEN TO GO	See roadside flowers in early June or the cranberry harvest in October.
CONNECTS WITH	Fort-to-Fort Trail, page 110

THIS ROUTE along the gentle hills east of Langley takes you through rolling farmland and tucked-away neighbourhoods before descending to the Fraser River.

After the first rise, on 240th Street, comes a peaceful interlude along a section of historic Telegraph Trail, once part of an

Stopping to smell the roses

overland telegraph route begun in 1865 to link Russia to the United States—a project doomed by the laying of a communications cable beneath the Atlantic Ocean the following year.

After a steep, winding descent to the floor of the valley, you'll see land being used for cranberry production. This is not as innovative as you might think: During the 1850s, cranberries harvested by Native peoples were packed at Fort Langley to be sent to San Francisco.

Glen Valley Regional Park includes Duncan, Poplar and Two-Bit Bars. At Poplar Bar, our suggested picnic spot, you can rest or enjoy your lunch on the riverbank. Opposite is Crescent Island. The Fraser River sweeps around it, bearing tugs, fishboats and debris; geese and goldeneye brave the current. Amid the turbid water, millions of migrating salmon travel up or downstream according to their season. Two-Bit Bar, reached at 24.7 kilometres, is notable for Hassall House, dating back to 1917. The house stands on rental property and is not open to the public.

Whether you cycle the Trans Canada Trail along Nathan Creek or choose the shorter option, take time to browse among Fort Langley's tea rooms, craft shops and antiques stores or visit the restored Hudson's Bay Company fort and adjacent museums.

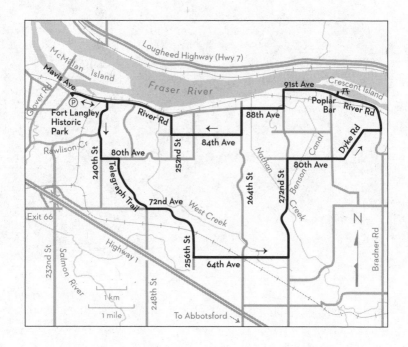

KM THE ROUTE

0.0 Fort Langley National Historic Park parking lot on Mavis Avenue.

0.2 Right on River Road.

1.8 Right on 240th Street.

3.2 Stay left on 240th Street at the junction with Rawlison Crescent.

4.1 Left on 80th Avenue.

4.7 Right on Telegraph Trail. Historic route.

6.8 Left on 72nd Avenue, which becomes 72nd Diversion.

8.6 Right on 256th Street.

9.7 Left on 64th Avenue.

11.4 Cross 264th Street at the stop sign.

13.0 Left on 272nd Street. Steep, winding descent—try not to fly past your next turning!

16.5 Right on 80th Avenue, which becomes Marsh-McCormick Road. Cranberry bogs.

Cross Lefeuvre Road.

18.6 Left on Dyke Road, which becomes Gray Avenue.

Llama stepping out

20.2 Left on Bradner Road.

21.0 Left on River Road. Optional hiking/cycling path along the riverbank leads to Poplar Bar.

22.8 Right at the gate to Poplar Bar, Glen Valley Regional Park. Picnic tables, toilets, information kiosk.

22.8 Continue west on River Road, which becomes 91st Avenue.

24.7 Two-Bit Bar is on the bend. Historic building, river view, toilets.

25.4 Right on 88th Avenue.

OPTION: To include a section of the Trans Canada Trail along Nathan Creek dyke, go straight ahead on 272nd Street. Turn right on 80th Avenue and continue to its end. Follow the dyke path northward to 88th Avenue. This diversion will add 3 km to your route.

Otherwise, continue on 88th Avenue to

26.8 Left on 264th Street.

27.6 Right on 84th Avenue. Fort Winery ahead on your right. Free tours and wine tasting.

29.1 Cross 256th Street.

29.9 Right on 252nd Street.

30.7 Left on River Road.

34.6 Left on Mavis Avenue.

34.9 Fort Langley National Historic Park parking lot.

> 28 **CAMPBELL RIVER VALLEY**

Langley

. . . . .

ROUND TRIP	26.7 km (16 ¾ miles)
TERRAIN	Paved roads and unpaved paths; rolling hills
TRAFFIC VOLUME	Low to moderate; may be busy on 16th Avenue
ALLOW	2 ½ to 3 ½ hours
HIGHLIGHTS	Country roads among farms and stables; Campbell Valley Regional Park: visitor centre, Annand/Rowlatt farmhouse, Lochiel school-house, wildlife garden; Noel Booth Park
PICNIC SPOT	Campbell Valley Regional Park (south entrance) at 13.8 km
STARTING POINT	Roadside parking at Noel Booth Community Park on 36th Avenue, or in the parking lot
HOW TO GET THERE	BY CAR: From Fraser Highway (Hwy 1A) or Hwy 1 exit 58, drive south on 200th Street. Turn left (east) on 36th Avenue.
	BY TRANSIT: Take the bus to 200th Street at 36th Avenue and ride to the starting point.
WHEN TO GO	Late August to pick blackberries in the park.

OUR ROUTE jogs southward in easy stages, taking you through quiet residential neighbourhoods and past eclectic hobby farms and horse paddocks.

Here and there among Langley's gentle hills stand old barns, split-rail fences and skeletal remnants of orchards—memorials to the region's pioneer farmers. One of the earliest settlers in this

Old barn near Langley

valley was Alexander Annand, whose restored 1898 homestead stands in Campbell Valley Regional Park. Nearby, the one-room Lochiel schoolhouse has come to rest in the park after having been moved three times and having done duty as a community hall.

The park's uplands and wetlands surrounding the Campbell River provide habitat for many varied animals, birds and plants. Cycling is not permitted in the park, but nature lovers can lock their bikes to the cycle rack and explore on foot. The Campbell River (more correctly, the Little Campbell River) takes a northward swing through the valley, thereby meeting your path once again before resuming its westward journey to Semiahmoo Bay.

KM	THE ROUTE

0.0	Noel Booth Community Park. East on 36th Avenue.
0.8	Right on 205th Street.
1.6	Right on 32nd Avenue.
1.8	Left on 204th Street. Lakes are visible on the left.
3.4	Jog left on 24th Avenue.
3.6	Right on 204A Street.
	Left on 20th Avenue.
5.1	Right on 208th Street.
5.9	Left on 16th Avenue. Busy main road.
6.7	Right on 212th Street. Go uphill, then down a longer hill.
8.4	Left on 8th Avenue.
9.2	Right on 216th Street. Cross Little Campbell River.
10.0	Right on 4th Avenue. Go gradually uphill.
	Right on 204th Street.
	Left on 8th Avenue.
13.4	Right to Campbell Valley Regional Park. Follow the driveway to the second parking lot.

13.8	Information kiosk; picnic tables to right, past washroom building; visitor centre; wildlife garden; walking trails. Cycling is not permitted in the park.
14.3	Left on 8th Avenue at the park entrance and retrace your inward route via 204th Street and 4th Avenue.
17.6	Left on 216th Street. Hills.
20.4	Left on 18th Avenue.
21.2	Right on 212th Street.
21.5	Left on 20th Avenue. Where the pavement ends, continue through the gate onto Fernridge Trail.
22.3	Cross 208th Street and continue west on 20th Avenue.
22.9	Right on 204A Street.
23.7	Left on 24th Avenue.
23.8	Right on 204th Street immediately before the bridge over Campbell River.
24.6	Left on 28th Avenue.
25.0	Right on 202nd Street. Continue beyond "No Exit" sign.

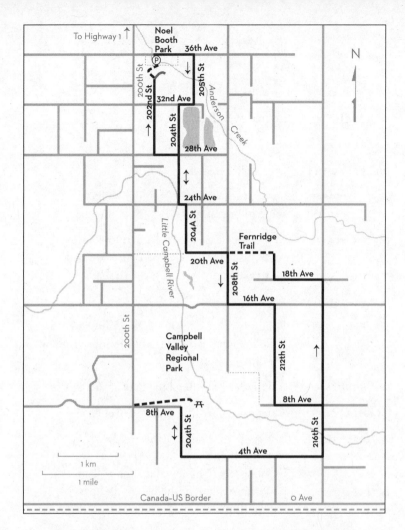

26.2 Where 202nd Street bends right, leave the pavement and follow the path beyond the concrete barriers. Keeping the fenced tennis courts on your right, cross a parking lot and road and enter Noel Booth Park through the gate opposite.

Continue past the baseball diamond and turn right across the bridge over Anderson Creek. Follow the gravel path to the left, skirting the sports field.

26.7 Noel Booth Community Park parking lot.

> 29 ALDERGROVE

Langley/Abbotsford

. . . . .

ROUND TRIP	25.3 km (16 miles)
TERRAIN	Paved roads and gravel trail; some flat, some rolling hills
TRAFFIC VOLUME	Moderate; heavy around Aldergrove. Gravel trucks use 8th Avenue and Lefeuvre Road on weekdays.
ALLOW	2 ½ to 3 ½ hours
HIGHLIGHTS	Roadside berry stalls in season, Aldergrove Lake Regional Park, views of Mount Baker and the Golden Ears
PICNIC SPOT	Aldergrove Lake Regional Park at 16.7 km
STARTING POINT	Aldergrove City Park on 32nd Avenue
HOW TO GET THERE	BY CAR: From Fraser Highway (Hwy 1A), turn north on 264th Street (Hwy 13), then immediately right on 32nd Avenue. Enter the park after 1.5 km, immediately after passing the sports field.
	BY TRANSIT: Take the bus to Fraser Highway (Hwy 1A) at 272nd Street and ride to the starting point.
WHEN TO GO	Attend the Aldergrove Fall Fair in September; sample local berries in June.

ALDERGROVE, A town known for tasty German sausages, also boasts a telephone museum and one of the oldest agricultural fairs in B.C. Leaving its small city park, you bowl

Borderline refreshments

along the hills and dales of southeastern Langley, passing tree nurseries and berry farms interspersed with paddocks and stables— evidence of Langley Township's claim to be "The Horse Capital of B.C."

A short stretch along the 49th parallel brings you to Aldergrove Lake Regional Park. This area is rich in gravel deposits left by retreating glaciers; the park's lake and ponds have been created from reclaimed gravel pits—work that is still going on. Unfortunately, the popular swimming lake, which was artificially created, has fallen into disrepair and is in danger of being permanently closed.

Much of the park is wooded and criss-crossed with a network of walking and equestrian trails, some of which are now open to cyclists. Park maps are available at the lake. Your route includes a stretch of the multi-use Rock'n Horse Trail, playfully named for a giant glacial erratic boulder along the way. This section is manageable by most bicycles, but if yours is a light-framed road bike, you may prefer to complete the ride on paved roads by continuing east from the park entrance on 8th Avenue to rejoin the described route at Lefeuvre Road. In this case, your distances from the intersection with Lefeuvre will be approximately 2 kilometres shorter than those given.

0.0 Aldergrove City Park parking lot. Left (east) on 32nd Avenue. The telephone museum is on the corner of 271st Street.

0.2 Right on 272nd Street.

1.9 Right on 24th Avenue.

5.2 Left on 256th Street. Undulating road. Pass several stables.

10.0 Left on 0 Avenue. This road runs along the Canada–U.S. border. There are raspberry farms and nurseries on your left. Continue to where 0 Avenue bends left to cross Hwy 13.

12.2 Cross Hwy 13 north of the border crossing and continue on 0 Avenue. Boundary Road in the U.S. runs parallel on your right.

13.6 Left on 272nd Street. Your climb is gradual, becoming steeper after the bend. Pass Equestrian Trailhead.

15.5 Right on 8th Avenue, then right at the park entrance 200 metres ahead. Follow the park access road, pass a sheltered picnic area in the field and turn right after the bridge into the main parking lot.

16.7 Aldergrove Lake. Picnic tables, bike rack, toilets, trail maps. Turn left past the lakeside picnic tables and follow the shared trail until you come to the signposted Rock'n Horse Trail.

16.9 Left on Rock'n Horse Trail. Ups and downs. Cyclists give way to pedestrians and horseback riders.

17.5 Keep right where the trail forks.

17.8 Left at the T-junction after a sharp rise. (Right leads to a good viewpoint in 50 m.)

17.9 Keep right on Rock'n Horse Trail at the next junction. Continue east along the avenue of alders, Pepin Brook visible below. Turn left through the parking lot to Lefeuvre Road.

18.4 Left on Lefeuvre Road. Hills. Cross Huntingdon Road and King Road.

22.6 Left on Swensson Avenue.

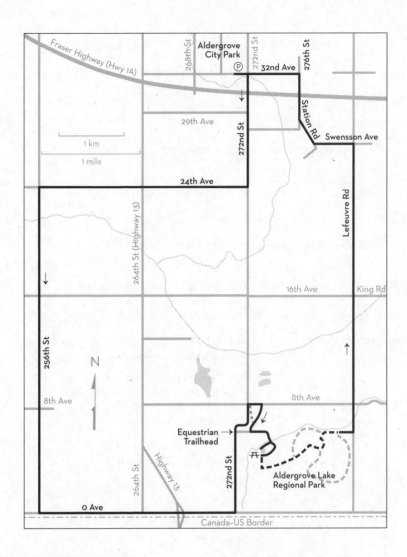

23.2 Right on Station Road.

23.6 Bear right on 276th Street
      and cross Fraser Highway
      (Hwy 1A) at the traffic light.

24.3 Left on 32nd Avenue.

25.3 Right into Aldergrove
      City Park.

> 30 MIRACLE VALLEY

Fraser Valley Regional District

. . . . .

ROUND TRIP	25.4 km (16 miles)
TERRAIN	Paved roads and short unpaved trail; some hills
TRAFFIC VOLUME	Low, possibly moderate on Sylvester Road
ALLOW	2 ½ to 3 ½ hours
HIGHLIGHTS	Farmlands and mountain views, Allen Lake, Cascade Creek and waterfall
PICNIC SPOT	Cascade Falls Regional Park at 11.4 km
STARTING POINT	Hatzic Prairie Community Hall on Farms Road
HOW TO GET THERE	BY CAR: From Lougheed Highway (Hwy 7) about 6.5 km east of Mission, turn left on Sylvester Road, then left on Farms Road. The community hall is at the junction of Farms and Dale Road.
	BY TRANSIT: There is no viable transit option at this time.
WHEN TO GO	Watch the cascades during spring run-off in June.

EXTENDING NORTHWARD from Hatzic Lake is a narrow valley criss-crossed by numerous creeks born in the mountain ramparts to the east. The route described takes you from the gentle farmlands of Hatzic Prairie to the sterner region through which Cascade Creek makes its helter-skelter descent. From our suggested picnic spot beside the creek, a foot trail climbs 90 metres to the spectacular double falls—an approach that is more in keeping with the spirit of the cascades than the gravel vehicle road.

Hatzic Prairie Market

On your return route to the prairie, Stave Lake Road provides a pleasing descent before passing through a quaintly rustic neighbourhood tucked against the western hillside. Rock climbers are often to be seen tackling the bluffs along here.

Be warned that a sudden thunderstorm in the Hatzic area is not uncommon, and while you may enjoy the sight and sound as it rolls around the surrounding mountains you'd be wise to keep rainwear handy on this outing.

0.0	Hatzic Prairie Community Hall parking lot. Left (north) on Farms Road.	11.4	Return on Ridgeview Road.
2.5	Straight ahead on Durieu Street after the bend.	12.2	Left on Sylvester Road.
		15.3	Right on Hartley Road. Steep hill.
3.2	Right on Seux Road. Straight ahead is a "No Thru Road" sign.	17.6	Left on Stave Lake Road. Ups and downs.
3.6	Left on Pattison Road.	20.9	Keep right on Stave Lake Road at the bend where Durieu Street goes left.
4.6	Left on Sylvester Road. This is a narrow, winding road with ups and downs.	21.4	Right to stay on Stave Lake Road. Watch closely for this turning, which is immediately before the bridge. Narrow, winding road.
	Pass Allen Lake on your left. There is no public access to the water.		
10.2	Cross the bridge over Cascade Creek.	24.2	Left on Dale Road.
10.6	Right on Ridgeview Road to Cascade Falls Regional Park.	25.4	Hatzic Prairie Community Hall at the junction with Farms Road. Refreshments available at Hatzic Prairie Market opposite.
11.4	Gate. The park is open year-round; you may walk in when the gate is closed (October to May). The gravel road continues to the top of the falls, but a gated track on the right leads to a picnic spot beside the creek, from which the cascades can be reached by a foot trail. Cycling is not allowed on the park trails.		

To Davis Lake

Cascade Falls
Regional Park

Ridgeview Rd

Sylvester Rd

Cascade Ck

Kontney Rd

Spratt Rd

Hartley Rd

Allen
Lake

Stave Lake Rd

Sylvester Rd

N

Durieu St

Seux Rd

Pattison Rd

Stave Lake Rd

Farms Rd

1 km

1 mile

P

Hatzic
Community Hall

Dale Rd

To Lougheed Highway (Hwy 7)

> 31 NICOMEN ISLAND

Fraser River Regional District

. . . . .

ROUND TRIP	22 km (13 ¾ miles)
TERRAIN	Paved roads and gravel road; flat
TRAFFIC VOLUME	Low, except for a short stretch of Lougheed Highway
ALLOW	1 ½ to 2 ½ hours
HIGHLIGHTS	Quiet country roads, waterfowl in Nicomen Slough, Quaamitch Slough, old store in Deroche
STARTING POINT	On North Nicomen Road in Deroche. Park beside the railway tracks opposite Deroche Community Hall.
HOW TO GET THERE	BY CAR: Drive east from Mission on Lougheed Highway (Hwy 7) about 21 km to Deroche. Turn left onto North Nicomen Road immediately after the bridge.
	BY TRANSIT: There is no viable transit option at this time.
WHEN TO GO	May and June to see geese and goslings in the slough; winter to view bald eagles.

NICOMEN ISLAND is the largest of several islands encompassed by the Fraser River and Nicomen Slough. Despite being bisected by the Lougheed Highway, the island remains a sleepy backwater where the cyclist can pedal beside the wide, slow-moving slough and among the farms and berry fields. A dyke protects the island from encroachment by the Fraser River, but as its path is fairly rough and gated at frequent intervals, the winding Nicomen Island Trunk Road affords a more comfortable ride.

Nicomen Slough

We have not yet found the perfect picnic spot on Nicomen Island; instead, we load our bikes back onto the car and drive 15 kilometres east on Lougheed Highway (Hwy 7) to Kilby Provincial Park on Harrison Bay. Here, there are picnic tables behind the Kilby General Store Museum or a homestyle lunch in the Harrison River Tea Room. Kilby is not large enough for a grand tour, but you can cycle to the end of Kilby Road and back, or through the tiny settlement to the bay, where the Harrison River gathers itself before entering the narrow channel to the Fraser.

An alternative to the lazy outing described is to combine the Nicomen Island route with the Dewdney dyke. For this you must brave the Lougheed Highway west of the Nicomen Island Trunk Road turnaround point, cross the bridge over Nicomen Slough and immediately turn left onto River Road South. From there, another 9 kilometres of dyke and farm roads are yours to explore.

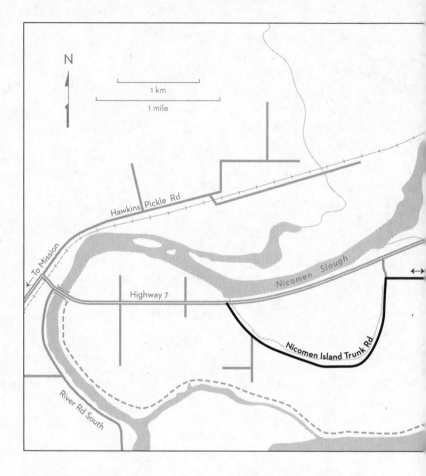

KM **THE ROUTE**

0.0   Deroche Community Hall. Right onto Lougheed Highway and cross the bridge over Nicomen Slough. Continue west on the highway—for a better view of the slough you can cycle on the dyke top, but return to the pavement before reaching the gate to private property.

3.5   Right on Ross Road, which becomes Nicomen Island Slough Road at the bend.

6.0   Left on Johnson Road.

Cross Lougheed Highway.

8.1   Right on Nicomen Island Trunk Road.

11.1   Turnaround point at the junction with Lougheed

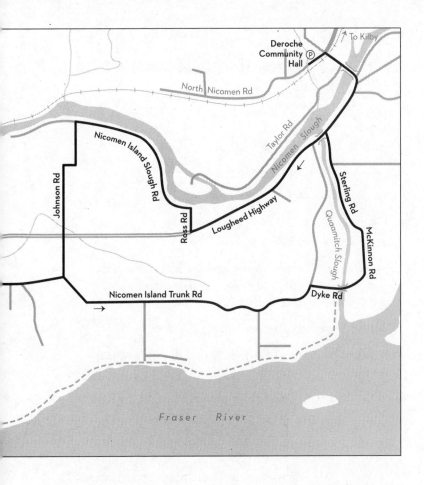

Highway. Retrace your route
on Nicomen Island Trunk
Road to avoid using the busy
highway.

14.1 Johnson Road on left. Stay
right to continue east on
Nicomen Island Trunk Road.

19.2 Right on Dyke Road. Cross
Quaamitch Slough.

19.9 Left on McKinnon Road,
which becomes Sterling
Road.

21.7 Right on Lougheed Highway.

Left on North Nicomen Road
after the bridge.

22.0 Deroche Community Hall.

> 32 HARRISON–AGASSIZ

Kent

. . . . .

ROUND TRIP	30.1 km (18 ¾ miles)
TERRAIN	Paved roads; flat
TRAFFIC	Low, except for Hot Springs Road (Hwy 9) and Agassiz
ALLOW	2 ½ to 3 ½ hours
HIGHLIGHTS	Harrison Hot Springs, mountain views, hazelnut groves, Agassiz-Harrison Museum, Old Agassiz Place, old Kent Municipal Cemetery
PICNIC SPOT	Pioneer Park in Agassiz at 18.2 km
STARTING POINT	Roadside parking on Lillooet Avenue in Harrison Hot Springs
HOW TO GET THERE	BY CAR: From Lougheed Highway (Hwy 7) or Hwy 1, take exit 135 and drive north on Hot Springs Road (Hwy 9) to Harrison Hot Springs.
	BY TRANSIT: If you are already in Chilliwack or Agassiz, catch Chilliwack/Agassiz-Harrison Transit Route 11: Agassiz-Harrison bus to the Harrison Hot Springs Hotel.
WHEN TO GO	Attend the Agassiz Fall Fair in September.

IF YOU'RE staying in Harrison Hot Springs, this easy ride through the Kent countryside makes a change from lake and beach activities. Ringed by mountains, the district of Kent was once a prime hop-growing area, taking its name from the English county of Kent famous for its hop fields. After the B.C. Hop Company moved to Creston in 1952, corn and dairying became the mainstays of Kent's economy.

Alpaca watching cyclists

After a rest in Pioneer Park and a saunter through the town, do allow time to visit the Agassiz-Harrison Museum and Visitor Centre now housed, complete with caboose, in the restored wooden Canadian Pacific Railway station on Pioneer Avenue. Artifacts and displays depict both the pioneer and rail history of the region. The museum is staffed by a band of dedicated volunteers, many of them descendants of local pioneering families. From the story of its earliest settlers, Thomas B. Hicks and Captain Lewis Agassiz, and the doings of Dr. McCaffrey (who tended his practice by riding the rails on a hand-propelled speeder) to an account of the 1948 Fraser Valley flood, when water surged through the town, Kent's lively history is lovingly preserved.

0.0	From Lillooet Avenue, go right (south) on Eagle Street.
0.8	Cross the Miami River. Eagle Street becomes McCombs Drive.
2.6	Right on McPherson Road.
2.9	Left on Hot Springs Road (Hwy 9).
3.8	Right on Golf Road, which becomes Hardy Road.
6.3	Right on McCallum Road, which becomes Cameron Road.
8.9	Cross Lougheed Highway (Hwy 7) and the railway tracks.
11.4	Left on Limbert Road. The road curves around the base of Cemetery Hill.
13.4	The old Kent cemetery lies on your left at the bend. A steep path leads uphill to the graves of Lewis Agassiz and his family.
	Limbert Road becomes Ashton Road.
14.4	Straight ahead on Pioneer Avenue where Ashton Road crosses the railway.
15.0	Right on Fir Road. Hopyard Hill lies on your right.
	Fir Road becomes Mountain View Road, with a view of Mount Cheam and its surrounding peaks.
16.5	Left on Agassiz Avenue. Built in 1867, Old Agassiz Place on your right was the home of the Agassiz family. The house is now a private residence.
17.7	Right on Pioneer Avenue.
18.2	Pioneer Park is on your left. Picnic tables. Agassiz-Harrison Museum and Visitor Centre.
18.2	Return west on Pioneer Avenue.
20.7	Right on Ashton Road and cross the railway tracks.
21.3	Left on Else Road, which becomes Birch Road.

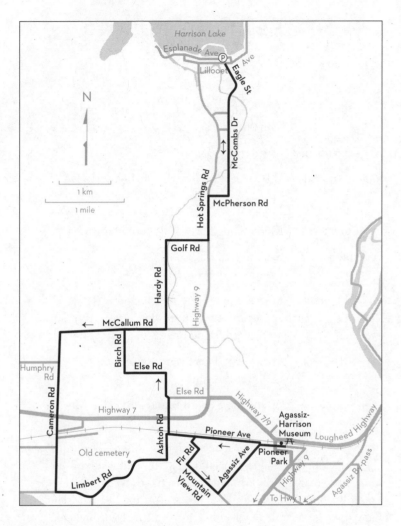

23.0 Right on McCallum Road.

23.8 Left on Hardy Road and retrace your outward route to Harrison via Golf Road, Hwy 9, McPherson Road and Eagle Street.

30.1 Lillooet Avenue, Harrison Hot Springs.

33

SEABIRD ISLAND

Kent

. . . . .

ROUND TRIP	14.3 km (9 miles) or 19.9 km (12 ½ miles) with optional side trip
TERRAIN	Paved roads; flat
TRAFFIC VOLUME	Low, except for Lougheed Highway (Hwy 7)
ALLOW	1 ½ to 2 hours
HIGHLIGHTS	Maria Slough, wetlands, mountain views
STARTING POINT	Seabird Island Road near the Community School
HOW TO GET THERE	BY CAR: From Lougheed Highway (Hwy 7), approximately 3 km east of Agassiz, turn left on Seabird Island Road.
	BY TRANSIT: There is no viable transit option at this time.
WHEN TO GO	Attend the Seabird Island Festival in May.

EAST OF Agassiz, the Lougheed Highway bisects Seabird Island, home of the Stó:lō First Nation. Established in 1879, the reserve comprises farmland and wetlands lying between the Fraser River and Maria Slough. The enterprising Seabird Island Band operates a cattle ranch, a nut grove, a truck stop and café, as well as running its own community school. Cyclists on Seabird Island Road will most likely get a friendly wave from residents.

We highly recommend the side trip on Chaplin Road. This country lane winds through a flat, narrow valley between the slopes of Bear Mountain and wide, peaceful Maria Slough. Returning (the road ends at a farmyard) you'll have a grand view of Mount Cheam rising to 2100 metres above the valley.

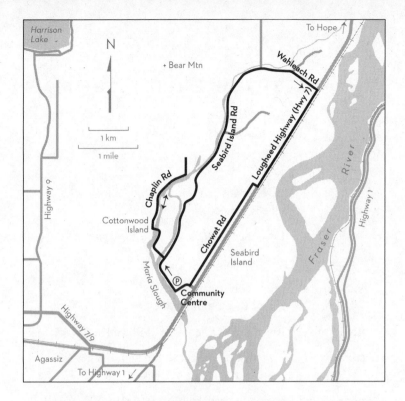

Although we have not specified a picnic spot on this short ride, perhaps you'll discover a suitable place, or load your bikes on to the car and head for Pioneer Park in Agassiz.

KM   THE ROUTE

0.0   Seabird Island Road near the Community School.

0.9   OPTION: Left on Chaplin Road takes you along the north side of Maria Slough to a turnaround point at Riverwyk Farm. Otherwise,

0.9   Continue on Seabird Island Road through the reserve. The road eventually becomes Wahleach Road.

8.1   Right onto Lougheed Highway.

10.8   Right on Chowat Road. Cycle behind the buildings to find the road; it runs parallel to the highway and will take you past Seabird Island Community Centre to your starting point near the school.

14.3   Seabird Island Road.

34

BRADNER–MT. LEHMAN

Abbotsford

. . . . .

ROUND TRIP	35.2 km (22 miles)
TERRAIN	Paved roads and unpaved trail (a hybrid bike is best for this); some hills
TRAFFIC VOLUME	Low, except moderate on 58th Avenue
ALLOW	3 ½ to 4 ½ hours
HIGHLIGHTS	Quiet country roads, daffodil fields, Fraser River, mountain views, Matsqui Trail
PICNIC SPOT	Riverbank at Glenmore Trailhead at 18.3 km
STARTING POINT	The west side of 264th Street, immediately north of the Hwy 1 overpass
HOW TO GET THERE	BY CAR: Leave Hwy 1 at exit 73 and drive north on 264th Street to the north end of the overpass. Park on the wide shoulder.
	BY TRANSIT: There is no viable transit option at this time.
WHEN TO GO	March and April to see the daffodils.

SOME ROLLICKING ups and downs take you over the rolling Bradner plateau, which is famous for its fields of tulips and daffodils. Flowers have been grown here since 1914, when the Fatkin family planted the first bulbs. A few years later, the first Bradner Flower Show was held—an annual festival that continues to this day, around Easter.

After a plunge down to prairie level, you reach the Fraser River at Glenmore Trailhead, where a 3.5-kilometre extension of the Matsqui Trail (also the Trans Canada Trail) heads west through

View from Matsqui Trail West

Matsqui First Nation reserve lands. This is a challenging trail with many twists and turns and some stretches of loose gravel. Ride carefully and be prepared to give way to hikers and horse riders.

Returning to paved roads, you stay high above the Fraser River through Mount Lehman, enjoying fine views of the mountains north of Mission before picking up your outward route opposite Bradner General Store.

KM	THE ROUTE

0.0 264th Street immediately north of the Hwy 1 overpass. East on 56th Avenue. This is a wide road through the industrial area.

2.8 Right on Baynes Street.

3.3 Left on Myrtle Avenue.

3.9 Left on Lefeuvre Road, then immediately right to continue on Myrtle. Caution: There is a steep, winding descent followed by a right-hand bend and a sudden uphill.

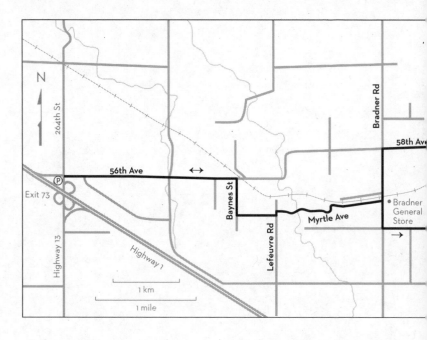

5.7 Right on Bradner Road.
The Bradner General Store
is opposite.

6.2 Left on Haverman Road.
Daffodil fields.

7.9 Right on Ross Road.

8.7 Left on Townshipline Road.
Daffodil fields.

10.3 Left on Mount Lehman Road.

11.2 Right on Hawkins Road.

11.9 Right on Olund Road. There
is a view of Matsqui Prairie
before the descent.

Left on Bates Road.

14.6 Right on Townshipline Road.

16.2 Left on Glenmore Road.
Cross Harris Road.

18.3 Cross the railway and ride to
the end of Glenmore. (Do
not take the gravel road to
the left.) To the right, a short
distance beyond the gate
onto the dyke, some rocks
provide a good picnic spot
with a view across the Fraser
River to Matsqui Island.

18.3 To continue, backtrack to the
sign "Matsqui First Nation
Reserve Lands" at the end
of Glenmore. Go west on
the Trans Canada Trail and
follow signs for 3.5 km. This
is a multi-use trail—please
ride carefully and give way
to walkers and horse riders.

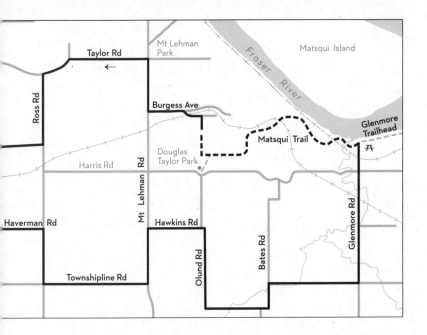

21.7 Keep straight ahead where a path branches left to Douglas Taylor Park parking lot.

21.8 Right at the T-junction onto the wood-chip trail. The trail rises steeply to join Olund Road.

Left at the T-junction. Cross the railway tracks and keep left on Burgess Avenue.

23.1 Right on Mount Lehman Road.

24.0 Left on Taylor Road. Views of mountains to the north.

25.6 Left on Ross Road.

27.2 Right on 58th Avenue. Busy road.

28.8 Left on Bradner Road.

29.5 Right on Myrtle Avenue opposite Bradner General Store.

Retrace your outward route, jogging left on Lefeuvre Road to continue on Myrtle Avenue.

32.4 Right on Baynes Street.

Left on 56th Avenue.

35.2 Left on 264th Street to parking area.

> 35 MATSQUI PRAIRIE

Abbotsford

. . . . .

ROUND TRIP	24.5 km (15 ½ miles)
TERRAIN	Paved roads and gravel dyke path; flat
TRAFFIC VOLUME	Low
ALLOW	2 ½ to 3 ½ hours
HIGHLIGHTS	Clayburn Village Store, quiet country roads, berry farms, Fraser River views, Matsqui Trail Regional Park
PICNIC SPOT	Mission Bridge Picnic Area at 16.5 km
STARTING POINT	Parking lot opposite Clayburn Village Store
HOW TO GET THERE	BY CAR: Leave Hwy 1 and drive north on Abbotsford-Mission Highway (Hwy 11), turn east on Clayburn Road and drive 2 km to Clayburn village.
	BY TRANSIT: If you are already in Abbotsford or Mission, take the Central Fraser Valley Transit Route 31: Valley Connector, get off on Hwy 11 at Clayburn Road and ride to the starting point.
WHEN TO GO	Buy local blueberries in August (and watch for scarecrows).

BETWEEN THE west side of Sumas Mountain and the Abbotsford-Mission Highway lies a pocket prairie. You'll cycle along quiet roads among berry patches and cornfields, fields of eggplants and red currants, dairy farms and poultry barns. In blueberry season, stylish scarecrows stand guard against raiding birds amid a cacophony of cannons and simulated hawk screams.

Stylish scarecrow

In due course, your route joins the Matsqui Trail (now part of
the Trans Canada Trail) along the south bank of the Fraser River.
From the gravel dyke path, you look out over riverside willows
to Westminster Abbey, perched on the hill above Mission. The
Mission Bridge Trailhead, our suggested picnic spot, offers an
unusual view of the bridge as well as a spacious picnic area and
other facilities.

Back at your starting point, tea with scones and Devonshire
cream at the Clayburn Village Store and Tea Shop is not to be
missed. This establishment, dating back to 1912, is a treasure house
of special goods—Fraser Valley jams, Melton Mowbray pies, bees-
wax polish from Aldergrove, an entire wall of British sweets and all
manner of memorabilia from bowler hats to biscuit tins. (Note that
the store is closed on Sundays and Mondays and all of January,
May and September.)

Before you load up your bike, take a ride around old Clayburn
village. It is the site of a brickyard, the Vancouver Fireclay
Company, established in the early 1900s with the discovery of good
fireclay on Sumas Mountain. Some of the company houses have
been restored, as has the church, which was meticulously rebuilt
brick by brick.

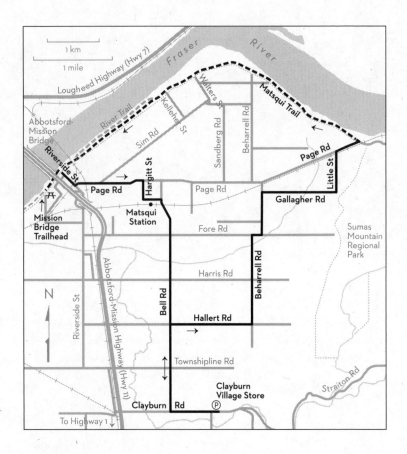

THE ROUTE

0.0 Clayburn Village Store. Go west on Clayburn Road.

1.0 Right on Bell Road. Blueberry farms.

Continue on Bell Road after the 4-way stop.

2.6 Right on Hallert Road.

4.2 Left on Beharrell Road.

5.8 Right on Fore Road at the microwave tower.

6.0 Left on Beharrell Road.

6.8 Right on Gallagher Road.

8.2 Left on Little Street.

8.9 Right on Page Road.

9.4 Left onto the dyke path. Matsqui Trail Regional Park. Be prepared to share the trail with walkers and horse riders.

13.4 OPTION: Right on River Trail (also Trans Canada Trail) takes you on a shared and shady pathway with occasional river views, to rejoin the dyke just before the railway crossing.

15.9 Cross the railway tracks and descend to the picnic area beyond Riverside Street.

16.5 Mission Bridge Picnic Area.

16.7 South on Riverside Street.

17.3 Left on Page Road.

18.7 Right on Hargitt Street. Follow the paved road left before the railway tracks. Matsqui Station is on your right.

19.4 Right on Bell Road.

23.5 Left on Clayburn Road.

24.5 Parking lot opposite the Clayburn Village Store.

> 36 SUMAS RIVER–BARROWTOWN

Abbotsford/Chilliwack

. . . . .

ROUND TRIP	31.3 km (19 ½ miles)
TERRAIN	Paved roads, unpaved dyke and trail; flat
TRAFFIC VOLUME	Low, except moderate on No. 3 Road
ALLOW	3 to 4 ½ hours
HIGHLIGHTS	Sumas River, McDonald Park, Vedder Canal, Great Blue Heron Nature Reserve, fruit and vegetable stalls
PICNIC SPOT	Great Blue Heron Nature Reserve at 17.3 km
STARTING POINT	McKay Creek Trail parking area on Eldridge Road
HOW TO GET THERE	BY CAR: Leave Hwy 1 at exit 95 (Whatcom Road), go left over the overpass and turn right on North Parallel Road, which becomes Eldridge Road. McKay Creek Trail parking area is on the west side of Sumas River before the road crosses a bridge.
	BY TRANSIT: There is no viable transit option at this time.
WHEN TO GO	Buy local vegetables and corn in July and August.
CONNECTS WITH	Vedder River, page 156

South lagoon, Great Blue Heron Nature Reserve

OUR ROUTE for this outing largely keeps company with the Trans Canada Trail along the waterways of Sumas Prairie. After a peaceful beginning beside the Sumas River, you arrive at McDonald Park, which is tucked against Sumas Mountain. Because the proximity of the mountain helps to block out artificial light, resulting in a particularly dark night sky, the park is a designated Dark Sky Preserve, from which astronomers have a clear view of the constellations.

Ahead, you'll pass the Barrowtown Pump Station which, together with the Vedder Canal, protects the surrounding farmland from the Fraser River's spring freshet. From the dyke atop the canal, the prairie unfolds before you, a patchwork of pasture, cornfields and tracts of vegetables.

A diversion on the Rotary Trail leads you to the Vedder River, here unrestrained by dykes, which you follow upstream to the wondrous world of the Great Blue Heron Nature Reserve. After rest and refreshment, take time to visit the Rotary Interpretive Centre before setting off homeward along the farm roads.

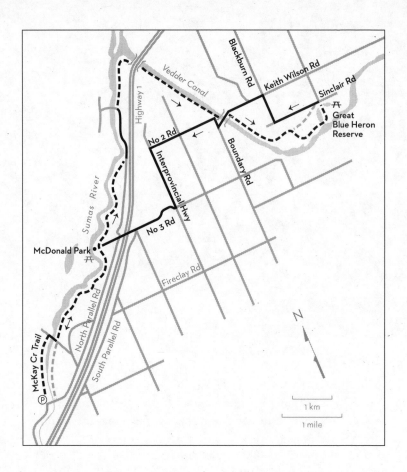

KM THE ROUTE

0.0 McKay Creek Trail parking area. The trail begins from the corner of the parking area. Sumas River is on your right.

1.7 After passing below a residence, go right across the bridge then left onto the dyke path.

4.7 McDonald Park. Picnic tables, toilets. Continue northeast along the dyke path.

7.3 Left onto North Parallel Road at the end of the dyke.

8.5 Barrowtown Pump Station. Left onto Quadling Road at the Trans Canada Trail sign, then sharp right onto the gravel dyke path.

10.5 Descend left to pass beneath Highway 1 on the rough track. Climb back to dyke level and continue alongside the Vedder Canal.

13.2 Keith Wilson Road bridge. Go left on the enclosed pathway. At the end of the pathway, cross Keith Wilson Road to enter a parking lot on the east side of the canal. Continue southeast on the dyke.

15.1 Leave the dyke (before the gate) and go right on the path beside a gravel storage site. Follow Rotary Trail West beside the Vedder River. This is a winding trail beneath tall cottonwoods with several bridges to cross.

16.6 Right at the junction with Heron Colony Trail (for walkers only), at the end of a bridge facing a lagoon and sluice.

16.7 Left through the gate onto the gravel road. Side paths lead to benches beside the lagoon. Pass a viewing tower and cross a wide bridge.

17.3 Great Blue Heron Nature Reserve and Rotary Interpretive Centre. Picnic tables, benches, natural history museum, gift shop, toilets, brochures, walking trails, volunteer staff on hand.

17.3 To continue, exit onto Sumas Prairie Road and immediately turn left on Sinclair Road.

18.6 Right on Blackburn Road.

19.4 Left on Keith Wilson Road.

20.7 After crossing Keith Wilson Road bridge (don't take the enclosed pathway) turn right at the T-junction onto Boundary Road, which becomes No. 2 Road.

22.9 Left on Interprovincial Highway.

24.4 Right on No. 3 Road. The Yellow Barn fruit and vegetable market is on your right. Use caution crossing the Highway 1 overpass.

26.6 McDonald Park. Retrace your outward route, with the option of staying on the upper dyke to the second bridge, where you cross the river to Eldridge Road and McKay Creek Trail.

31.3 McKay Creek Trail parking area.

> 37 SUMAS PRAIRIE

Abbotsford/Chilliwack

. . . . .

ROUND TRIP	36.8 km (23 miles)
TERRAIN	Paved roads and unpaved trail; mostly flat, one long hill
TRAFFIC VOLUME	Low, except moderate in Yarrow
ALLOW	3 ½ to 5 hours
HIGHLIGHTS	Spacious farmland with mountain views, Majuba Heritage Park, Saar Creek Trail, Hougen Park beside the Sumas River
PICNIC SPOT	Hougen Park at 23.5 km
STARTING POINT	Yarrow Central Park parking area on Kehler Street
HOW TO GET THERE	BY CAR: Travelling east, leave Hwy 1 at exit 104 and take No. 3 Road to Yarrow
	BY TRANSIT: There is no reliable transit option at this time (Chilliwack/Harrison-Agassiz Transit Route 8: Yarrow & Greendale services this route, but the buses are not always equipped with bicycle racks).
WHEN TO GO	Attend Yarrow Days during the first weekend in June.

MOST OF us have gazed at Sumas Prairie from a vehicle as we sped through the Fraser Valley on the highway. This varied bicycle route takes you to some little-known corners of that flat expanse: a tiny park on the Old Yale Wagon Road, a peaceful enclave not far from the Canada–U.S. border, a creekside

Picnic at Hougen Park

trail through farmers' fields, an inviting riverside park. From every corner, you can look up to the encircling mountains.

Once a 12 000-hectare lake, the rich farmland between Highway 1 and the U.S. border is the result of drainage and flood control measures during the 1920s. Mennonite families came from Russia and other parts of Canada to farm this corner of the newly created prairie. Today, the well-kept farms grow corn and other crops along with lush grass to feed milk-producing Holstein herds. Yarrow, at the foot of Vedder Mountain, serves the farming community and celebrates its Mennonite and pioneering history during Yarrow Days, when visitors can watch a colourful parade and sample local crafts and food.

0.0	Yarrow Central Park parking lot on Kehler Street. Right on Yarrow Central Road.	14.0	Right on Old Yale Road, which becomes Maher Road.
0.7	Right on Wilson Road.	18.4	Right on Lamson Road.

0.0 Yarrow Central Park parking lot on Kehler Street. Right on Yarrow Central Road.

0.7 Right on Wilson Road.

1.3 Majuba Heritage Park is on your left. Information booth with photographs and history of the Old Yale Wagon Road and stories of pioneer families.

Right on Majuba Hill Road. The road climbs in easy stages; the descent is steeper—use caution and be prepared for a railway crossing immediately after a bend at 5.9 km.

6.0 Left on Towne Road, which becomes Campbell Road.

7.7 Left on Interprovincial Highway, which becomes Wells Line Road.

10.5 Left on Powerhouse Road. The old powerhouse is visible ahead. Don't miss the Mootel and the Udder Barn!

12.1 Right on Vye Road.

12.9 Left on Marion Road.

14.0 Right on Old Yale Road, which becomes Maher Road.

18.4 Right on Lamson Road.

20.8 Left on Wells Line Road, then immediately right onto Saar Creek Trail. Stay on the dyke as it intersects farm tracks.

23.2 Left on Cole Road.

23.5 Left into Hougen Park. Riverside picnic tables, toilets.

23.5 Backtrack to Cole Road and continue south.

23.8 Left on Campbell Road.

28.0 Left on Dixon Road.

29.6 Right on No. 5 Road.

32.8 Left on Boundary Road.

33.6 Right on Sand Road.

34.7 Left on Stewart Road.

35.9 Right on Yarrow Central Road.

36.8 Right on Kehler Street to Yarrow Central Park parking lot.

> 38 VEDDER RIVER

Chilliwack

. . . . .

ROUND TRIP	23.7 km (14 ¾ miles)
TERRAIN	Paved roads, unpaved trail; mostly flat
TRAFFIC VOLUME	Low, except on Luckakuck Way and around Vedder Crossing
ALLOW	2 ½ to 3 ½ hours
HIGHLIGHTS	Rotary Vedder River Trail, Great Blue Heron Nature Reserve, rural Greendale, antique farm machinery exhibition
PICNIC SPOT	Great Blue Heron Nature Reserve at 14.8 km or on Rotary Vedder River Trail after 7.8 km
STARTING POINT	Chilliwack Visitor Centre, 44150 Luckakuck Way. Ask permission to leave your car if the centre is busy, or use the adjacent gravel parking area.
HOW TO GET THERE	BY CAR: Leave Hwy 1 at exit 116 (Lickman Road) and follow signs to the Chilliwack Visitor Centre.
	BY TRANSIT: There is no reliable transit option at this time (Chilliwack/Agassiz-Harrison Transit Route 7: Sardis via Higginson services this route, but not all of the buses are equipped with bicycle racks).
WHEN TO GO	See the Vedder River in full spate in June, or watch anglers line the banks during the salmon run in the fall.
CONNECTS WITH	Sumas River–Barrowtown, page 148

A FTER A straightforward run through the outskirts of Sardis, you will arrive at Vedder Crossing, where the water flows under the bridge as the Chilliwack River and out the other side as the Vedder River—a rechristening that took place early in the last century when the water was diverted into a new channel. On the estimable Rotary Trail, you cycle downstream beside an untamed river whose clear pools and whitewater runs are an angler's paradise. Rotary Trail users can enjoy the magnificent scenery and the wildflowers that adorn the riverbank.

Allow time at the Great Blue Heron Nature Reserve to look at the natural history displays and talk to the experienced volunteers who operate the centre. After lunching at the picnic tables behind the building, you can lock your bicycle to the rack and take one of the self-guided loop trails described in the brochure available at the centre. The reserve harbours one of the largest heron colonies in the Lower Mainland as well as a host of waterfowl, raptors and songbirds.

A final attraction on this interesting ride could be the exhibition of antique farm machinery, automobiles and steam engines at the Atchelitz Threshermen's site behind the visitor centre.

KM   THE ROUTE

0.0   Chilliwack Visitor Centre, Luckakuck Way.

Right (east) on Luckakuck Way.

1.7   Right at the sign to Evans Road.

4.4   Left on South Sumas Road, then immediately right onto Tyson Road.

6.0   Left on Keith Wilson Road.

7.0   Right on Vedder Road.

7.8   Right into the Rotary Vedder River Trail parking lot, just before the bridge.

Follow Rotary/Trans Canada Trail signs. After passing beneath the railway, go right onto the equestrian trail through the woods. Turn right at the gate to the Great Blue Heron Nature Reserve. A lagoon is on your left.

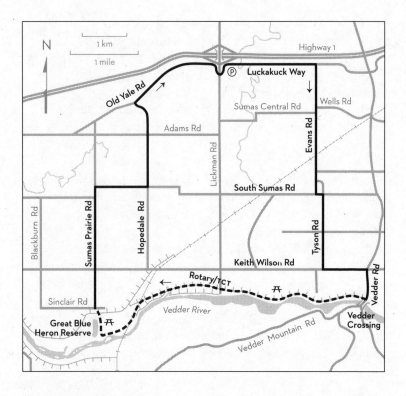

14.8 Cross the bridge and head
right to the Great Blue
Heron Nature Reserve
and Rotary Interpretive
Centre. Toilets, picnic
tables, brochures, nature
trails (walking only).

14.8 When it's time to leave,
go straight ahead (north) on
Sumas Prairie Road.

17.4 Right on South Sumas Road
in Greendale.

18.5 Left on Hopedale Road.

20.5 Right on Old Yale Road.

22.8 Cross Lickman Road onto
Luckakuck Way.

23.7 Chilliwack Visitor Centre.

39

COLUMBIA VALLEY

Fraser Valley Regional District

ROUND TRIP	11.3 km (7 miles) or 22.3 km (14 miles)
TERRAIN	Paved roads; some gentle hills
TRAFFIC VOLUME	Low
ALLOW	2 to 3 hours
HIGHLIGHTS	Peaceful countryside, pony farm, views across the U.S. border to International Ridge, historical plaque
PICNIC SPOT AND STARTING POINT	Columbia Valley Community Centre on Erho Road
HOW TO GET THERE	BY CAR: Leave Hwy 1 at exit 119 for Sardis and drive south following the signs to Cultus Lake. Continue on Columbia Valley Highway past Maple Bay and up the hill. Turn left on Kosikar Road and left to the community centre on Erho Road.
	BY TRANSIT: There is no viable transit option at this time.
WHEN TO GO	July and August for a swim in Cultus Lake.

TUCKED AWAY at the foot of International Ridge is an Arcadian plateau. Since the region can be reached only by a long, steep climb from the south end of Cultus Lake, we prefer to transport our bikes to the top, contenting ourselves with an easy ride the whole family can enjoy. To make the most of this miniature Eden, we usually do the longer route, which includes an extra loop.

In the grounds of the community centre, a plaque honours early pioneers. Until 1916, when a wagon road to the Chilliwack Valley was made, settlers in this valley had to cross the border into

Spotted mare and foal

Washington to get supplies. Today, as you cycle along the quiet
roads, there is a sense of having fallen into a time warp: speckled
hens scratch outside a cottage with beehives in the garden, sheep
and donkeys watch you pass, ponies and their foals gather by the
fence when you stop. Don't hurry or you'll break the spell.

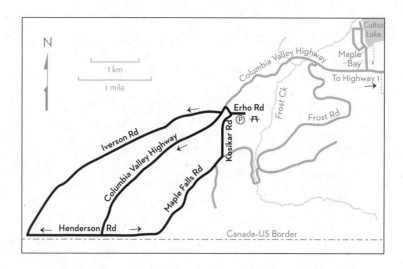

KM	THE ROUTE

0.0 Columbia Valley Community Centre. Right on Kosikar Road.

0.2 Left on Columbia Valley Highway.

0.4 Right on Iverson Road at the fork. Easy rolling hills.

5.4 Iverson becomes Henderson Road on the bend. You're now cycling along the international border. A 12-m-wide cut on the hillside opposite marks the boundary between the United States and Canada.

8.2 Henderson becomes Maple Falls Road.

10.3 Left on Kosikar Road.

11.3 Right is Erho Road and the community centre.

11.4 For a longer ride, continue left on Columbia Valley Highway.

11.6 Left at the fork. Columbia Valley Highway now passes through the centre of the valley.

15.3 Right and uphill on Henderson Road, which becomes Iverson Road.

21.9 Stay left on Iverson Road.

22.1 Right on Kosikar Road.

22.3 Left on Erho Road to Columbia Valley Community Centre.

40

FRASER RIVER ISLANDS

Chilliwack

· · · · ·

ROUND TRIP	33.6 km (21 miles)
TERRAIN	Paved roads; flat
TRAFFIC VOLUME	Low
ALLOW	3 to 4 hours
HIGHLIGHTS	Camp Slough, Hope Slough, winding roads, farms, nut groves, mountain views, heritage building
PICNIC SPOT	Kinsmen Park on Hope River Road at 19.7 km
STARTING POINT	Rosedale Community Park on Old Yale Road
HOW TO GET THERE	BY CAR: Leave Hwy 1 at exit 135 and drive north on Agassiz-Rosedale Highway (Hwy 9). Turn left (west) on Yale Road East to Rosedale. The park is at the junction of Yale Road East and Old Yale Road.
	BY TRANSIT: If you are already in Chilliwack, take the Chilliwack/Agassiz-Harrison Transit Route 11: Agassiz-Harrison, get off on Old Yale Road at McGrath Road and ride to the starting point.
WHEN TO GO	June or July for a shady ride and to see water lilies in the sloughs.

BETWEEN ROSEDALE and Chilliwack, the Fraser River flood plain is laced with sloughs that effectively carve the land into islands. Cycling is the perfect mode of travel for

Camp Slough

exploring these meandering waterways. There's time to watch the herons fishing and the ducks dabbling in green, willow-fringed Camp Slough and to notice the overhanging walnut trees and the huge old maples. The Fraser River dykes, too, offer good cycling, but for comfort and a variety of scenery, our route follows the paved roads in their wanderings over Rosebank, Windermere and Fairfield Islands.

Having reached the more serious Hope River Road and rested on the banks of Hope Slough, you can enjoy an easy run back to Rosedale among a fair sampling of Chilliwack's nine hundred farms. Mount Cheam and its sister peaks dominate the scene.

Several historic buildings lie along your route. On Jesperson Road, look for Jesperson House, built in 1912. Rosedale United Church on Yale Road East was built in 1908 for a cost of $125; its original steeple bell is still in use.

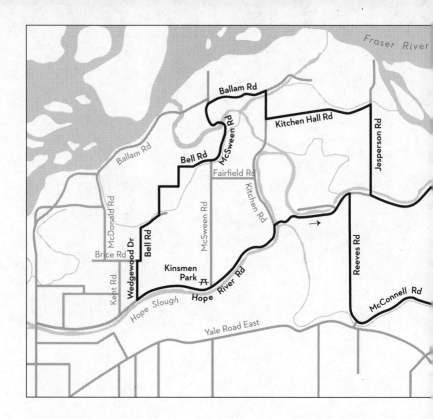

KM THE ROUTE

0.0 Rosedale Community Park. Right (north) on Old Yale Road.

0.8 Left on Bustin Road.

2.3 Left on Ferry Road. (Right goes to Ferry Island Provincial Park and Cheam First Nation reserve.) Ferry Road becomes Camp River Road. After passing Camp River Community Hall, watch for a row of heritage maple trees. Camp Slough is on your right.

9.9 Right on Jesperson Road. Cross Camp Slough.

11.3 Left on Kitchen Hall Road.

13.0 Right on Kitchen Road.

13.4 Left on Ballam Road.

14.3 Keep left on McSween Road where Ballam Road turns right.

15.7 Keep straight ahead on Bell Road. Enter the residential area.

Jog right on Brice Road, then

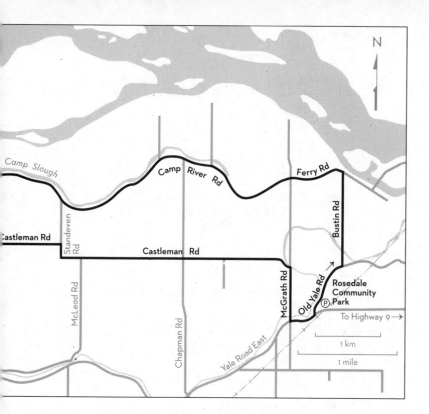

18.2 Left on Wedgewood Drive.

18.8 Left on Hope River Road.

19.7 Kinsmen Hall and park are on the right. Picnic tables beside Hope Slough.

19.7 Continue east on Hope River Road.

21.4 Right on Camp River Road. Cross Gravelly Slough.

22.8 Right on Reeves Road.

24.8 Keep straight ahead on McConnell Road where Reeves bends right to meet Yale Road East.

26.4 Left on Gillanders Road.

Right on Castleman Road at the bend.

28.4 Right on Standeven Road.

Left on Castleman Road at the bend.

32.3 Right on McGrath Road.

33.1 Left on Yale Road East.

33.6 Left on Old Yale Road to Rosedale Community Park.

> 41 POINT ROBERTS

Delta/Whatcom County, U.S.

. . . . .

ROUND TRIP	16.7 km (10 ½ miles)
TERRAIN	Paved roads, optional unpaved trail; mostly flat, one or two hills
TRAFFIC VOLUME	Low
ALLOW	2 to 3 hours
HIGHLIGHTS	Diefenbaker Park, Lily Point (optional), Lighthouse Marine Park, Monument Park, ocean views
PICNIC SPOT	Lighthouse Marine Park at 10.6 km
STARTING POINT	Diefenbaker Park, Tsawwassen
HOW TO GET THERE	BY CAR: Leave Hwy 99 South at exit 28 (Hwy 17), then go left on 56th Street to Tsawwassen. Continue south on 56th Street to Diefenbaker Park on the corner of 1st Avenue.
	BY TRANSIT: Take the bus to 54th Street at 2nd Avenue and ride to the starting point.
WHEN TO GO	Watch for pods of killer whales in the summer months.

A S THIS ride crosses the U.S. border, carry the required identification and medical insurance. Only a half-hour's drive from Vancouver, Point Roberts offers rural cycling with enough ports-of-call to please the whole family.

After meandering through the wooded central part of the peninsula, you might elect to take a side trip to Lily Point, the domain of eagles. From atop the bluff you look southward across the ocean toward the San Juan Islands.

Heading for the beach

Back on route, it's an easy run to Whatcom County's Lighthouse Marine Park at the southwest tip of the peninsula. Here you can explore rose-bordered trails among the sand dunes or enjoy a sheltered picnic on the boardwalk (leave your bikes below) or simply lean against driftwood on the beach and look out across the ruffled waters of the Strait of Georgia. Since strong currents and cold water are deterrents to swimming here, you might be content to watch for pods of killer whales or rafts of sea lions—both frequently spotted from this shore. Binoculars could be handy. To learn more about marine life, visit the park's interpretive centre, Orca House.

Don't miss tiny Monument Park on your way back to the border. Here stands Boundary Marker No. 1, the first in the long line of Canada–U.S. border markers across the continent. The obelisk was made in Scotland; its history and that of the 1846 Treaty of Washington are inscribed upon it.

Back at your starting point, take a stroll or a rest in Diefenbaker Park, a green oasis created from an abandoned quarry.

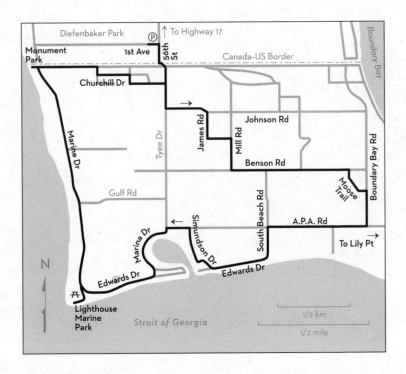

THE ROUTE

0.0 Diefenbaker Park. Left on 1st Avenue.

Right on 56th Street.

0.4 American Customs. After checking in, continue south on Tyee Drive.

1.1 Left on Johnson Road.

1.6 Right on James Road, which becomes Austin Road.

2.3 Right on Mill Road.

2.7 Left on Benson Road.

4.1 Right on Moose Trail.

4.7 Right on Boundary Bay Road.

5.1 T-junction at A.P.A. Road.

OPTION: For a side trip to Lily Point, turn left on A.P.A. Road, pass a small cemetery and follow the trail to its end at a fenced viewpoint. Add about 3 km for this side trip. Otherwise go right on A.P.A. Road.

6.3 Left on South Beach Road.

6.8 Bear right on Edwards Drive. There is unofficial beach access at the foot of South Beach Road—view across the Strait of Georgia to the San Juan Islands.

Edwards Drive becomes Simundson Drive. Point Roberts Marina is on your left. Café, public toilets on the access road beyond the boatyard.

8.3 Left on A.P.A. Road.

8.6 Left at the T-junction onto Marina Drive. The road curves around a sheltered marina.

9.6 Bear right onto Edwards Drive.

10.6 Left into Lighthouse Marine Park. Picnic tables, toilets, beach, campsites.

10.6 Continue north on Marine Drive. Pass Point Roberts Golf and Country Club.

14.2 Monument Park. View of Tsawwassen ferry terminal and Roberts Bank coal port.

Continue east on Roosevelt Way.

14.9 Right on Winston Drive.

15.0 Left on Churchill Drive.

15.4 Right on Delano Way, which becomes McKenzie Way.

16.0 Left on Tyee Drive.

16.3 Join the traffic to pass through Canadian Customs.

16.5 Left on 1st Avenue.

16.7 Diefenbaker Park.

> 42 NOOKSACK VALLEY—FERNDALE

Whatcom County, U.S.

. . . . .

ROUND TRIP	45.1 km (28 miles)
TERRAIN	Paved roads; a few hills
TRAFFIC VOLUME	Low, except in Lynden and Ferndale
ALLOW	3 ½ to 4 ½ hours
HIGHLIGHTS	Dutch Village in Lynden, farms, orchards, views of Mount Baker, Pioneer Park in Ferndale, Hovander Homestead Park (optional)
PICNIC SPOT	Pioneer Park at 22.6 km
STARTING POINT	Lynden City Park on Depot Road (3rd Street)
HOW TO GET THERE	BY CAR: Cross the U.S. border on Hwy 13 and continue south on Guide Meridian Road (SR 539). Turn left on East Badger Road and right on Depot Road. The park is on the left after 1.7 km.
	BY TRANSIT: The best option is to begin and end the ride at Ferndale. Take the bus to King George Boulevard at 8th, cross the border and catch Whatcom Transit Authority Route 55 to Ferndale.
WHEN TO GO	Late July to attend the Old Settlers' Picnic in Pioneer Park.
CONNECTS WITH	Nooksack Valley—Everson, page 174

General store, Pioneer Park

A S THIS ride begins south of the U.S. border, carry the required identification and medical insurance. This longer ride from Lynden into the Nooksack Valley has for its destination a charming pioneer village. Eleven log cabins, all more than a hundred years old, have been moved from their original sites around Whatcom County and arranged in a village setting beside the Nooksack River in Ferndale. A church, general store, post office, schoolhouse and several homes, complete with contents, are there for your inspection. Costumed volunteer staff members are on hand to answer questions and add to the atmosphere of bygone days. If you visit in late July, you can join in the Old Settlers' Picnic, an annual community event held in the village.

Adding to the pioneer flavour of this outing is the Nooksack Valley's Dutch heritage, evident in the farms along the route and exemplified in the town of Lynden. (See the Nooksack Valley—Everson ride on page 174.)

An added attraction near Ferndale is Hovander Homestead Park. The beautifully restored farmhouse, surrounded by flower beds and an herb garden, was built in 1901 by immigrant Swedish architect Hakan Hovander. To reach this destination from East Main Street (east of the Nooksack River) in Ferndale, turn south on Hovander Road then right onto Neilson Avenue. The side trip adds about 6 kilometres to the ride described. The county park is open year-round; Hovander House is open Fridays through Sundays in summer.

0.0 Lynden City Park.

Left on 3rd Street (Depot Road).

0.6 Left on Main Street.

0.9 Right on 1st Street, which becomes Hannegan Road.

2.0 Cross the bridge over the Nooksack River and continue on Hannegan Road.

4.7 Right on van Dyk Road.

Left on Huisman Road.

5.9 Right on East Wiser Lake Road. Winding road. Pass Wiser Lake on your left.

Cross Guide Meridian Road (SR 539) at the roundabout. Use caution.

12.4 Left on Woodlyn Road. Raspberry fields.

15.5 Right on Piper Road.

16.2 Left on Northwest Drive.

17.3 Right on Paradise Road. This is a winding road with ups and downs.

19.9 Left on Barrett Road.

20.8 Right on Main Street. Heavy traffic entering Ferndale.

Cross I-5. Caution: Very narrow shoulder for cyclists.

Go underneath the railway, then bear right and cross the Nooksack River. Note the sign: "Pioneer Park Left."

22.3 Left on 1st Avenue.

22.6 Cherry Street. Pioneer Park ahead. Pioneer village, picnic tables, toilets.

22.6 Left on Cherry Street.

22.7 Right on 3rd Avenue.

23.0 Cross Main Street, then cross Vista Drive.

23.7 Right on Washington Street.

23.9 Left on 2nd Avenue.

25.0 Right at the roundabout to Portal Way, through the I-5 underpass. Continue on Portal Way.

27.5 Straight ahead on Enterprise Road where Portal Way bends left.

Cross Grandview Road.

30.7 Right on Harksell Road.

31.3 Left on North Enterprise Road.

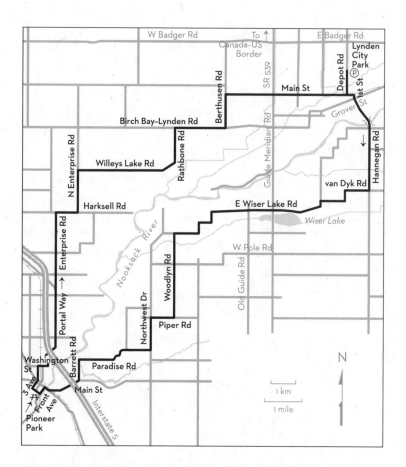

32.9 Right on Willeys Lake Road.
Lake and orchards. The road
becomes Rathbone Road.

37.7 Right on Birch Bay–
Lynden Road.

39.4 Left on Berthusen Road.

40.6 Right on West Main Street.

Cross Guide Meridian
Road (SR 539).

44.7 Left on 3rd Street
(Depot Road).

45.1 Right into Lynden
City Park.

> 43 NOOKSACK VALLEY—EVERSON

Whatcom County, U.S.

. . . . .

ROUND TRIP	27.7 km (17 ¼ miles)
TERRAIN	Paved roads; mostly flat
TRAFFIC VOLUME	Low, except moderate in Lynden and Everson
ALLOW	2 to 3 hours
HIGHLIGHTS	Dutch Village in Lynden, Pioneer Museum, Nooksack River, farms and country roads, views of Mount Baker, Fishtrap Creek
PICNIC SPOT	Riverside Memorial Park in Everson at 13.1 km
STARTING POINT	Lynden City Park on Depot Road (3rd Street)
HOW TO GET THERE	BY CAR: Cross the U.S. border on Hwy 13 and continue south on Guide Meridian Road (SR 539). Turn left on East Badger Road and right on Depot Road. The park is on the left after 1.7 km.
	BY TRANSIT: There is no convenient transit option available at this time.
WHEN TO GO	See the Nooksack River during its spring run-off during June.
CONNECTS WITH	Nooksack Valley—Ferndale, page 170

A S THIS ride begins south of the U.S. border, carry the required identification and medical insurance. Lynden is such a delightful town that you may find it best, for the sake of the ride, to leave immediately by the back door and save the town's

Dutch Village, Lynden

attractions for your return. Then you can stroll at leisure beneath the oak trees on Front Street, sample coffee and pastries in the Dutch Village, or visit the Pioneer Museum to see a replica of a 1900s farmhouse and a collection of vintage cars and wagons.

The Nooksack River flood plain was dyked and settled by Dutch immigrant farmers. Today, as you cycle past the well-tended farms—many with Dutch names on their mailboxes—glossy Holstein cows raise their heads to watch you pass. At Everson, your turnaround point, the Nooksack River slides placidly past the cottonwoods at Riverside Park—unless you are there during spring run-off, when temporary fencing reminds you to stay well back from the swollen torrent.

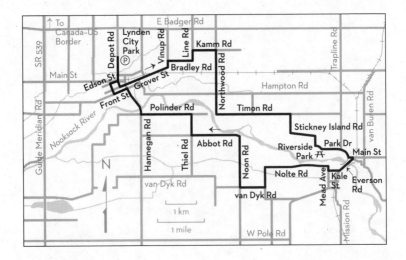

KM **THE ROUTE**

0.0 Lynden City Park. Left on 3rd Street (Depot Road).

Cross Main Street.

0.7 Left on Grover Street.

Cross 1st Street at the 4-way stop.

2.8 Right on Bradley Road. School on corner.

3.6 Left on Line Road.

4.0 Right on Kamm Road.

4.8 Right on Northwood Road.

Left on Timon Road.

9.8 Right on Stickney Island Road.

12.6 Stickney Island Road becomes Park Drive.

13.1 Right into Riverside Memorial Park. Picnic tables beside the Nooksack River, toilets.

13.2 Right on Park Drive, which becomes Main Street, entering Everson.

13.4 Right over bridge across Nooksack River. Use the sidewalk if traffic is heavy.

At the end of the bridge, continue straight ahead onto Kale Street.

14.5 Right on Mead Avenue, which becomes Nolte Road.

17.7 Right on van Dyk Road (not straight on).

18.5 Right on Noon Road, which becomes Abbot Road. There is a good view of the river from the top of the embankment.

22.2 Right on Thiel Road.

23.1 Left on Polinder Road.

24.7 Right on Hannegan Road and over the bridge. Busy main road.

25.8 Left on Front Street. Busy intersection—it is best to walk your bike in the crosswalks. You are now entering the historic district of Lynden. Visit the Dutch Village and the Pioneer Museum at the corner of Front and 3rd Streets.

26.5 Right on 7th Street.

26.8 Right on Edson Street.

27.2 Right on Main Street then immediately left on 3rd Street (Depot Road).

27.7 Right into Lynden City Park. Paths beside Fishtrap Creek.

> 44 SUMAS RIVER

Chilliwack/Whatcom County, U.S.

. . . . .

ROUND TRIP	35.2 km (22 miles)
TERRAIN	Paved roads; mostly flat, some gentle hills
TRAFFIC VOLUME	Low, except for Huntingdon–Sumas border crossing
ALLOW	3 to 4 hours
HIGHLIGHTS	Farms, orchards, mountain views, Sumas River, Nooksack City Park
PICNIC SPOT	Nooksack City Park at 17.6 km
STARTING POINT	Vicinity of Upper Sumas Elementary School on Whatcom Road
HOW TO GET THERE	BY CAR: Leave Hwy 1 at exit 95 and drive south on Whatcom Road to Vye Road. The school is on the corner. Please be considerate if parking during school hours—there is plenty of space at the roadside. BY TRANSIT: If you are already in Abbotsford, take the Central Valley Transit Route 2: Bluejay–Huntingdon GoLine bus to Sumas Way (Hwy 11) at Vye Road and ride to the starting point (or get off at 4th Avenue and B Street and begin your ride at the border).
WHEN TO GO	See cattle in the fields and activity on the farms in July and August.

City Park sign

As THIS ride crosses the border, carry the required identification and medical insurance. Along this route, which begins on Sumas Prairie and continues through the lush farmland in the shadow of Sumas Mountain in Whatcom County, you will cross the Sumas River several times. The wandering watercourse, however, is easily overlooked as it slips along between grassy banks and overhanging bushes. There are sequestered corners where gardens flourish around well-kept homes and wide views across fields of corn to the foothills of Mount Baker.

To the drivers of cars, trucks and milk tankers on State Route 9, the town of Nooksack is passed in a flash, but as you cycle by you'll notice the fine school on the hill, the homely post office building and the handsome sign announcing the city park. This sliver of land between road and railway offers picnic tables beneath a stand of beautiful Douglas-firs and maples.

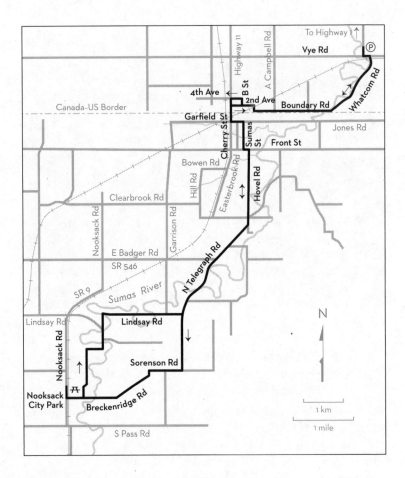

KM   **THE ROUTE**

0.0   Upper Sumas Elementary School. Left (east) on Vye Road.

0.2   Right on Whatcom Road and cross the railway. The Sumas River is on your right. Whatcom Road becomes Boundary Road, then

changes to 2nd Avenue at the bend by the lumberyard.

5.1   Right on B Street.

5.3   Left on 4th Avenue.

5.4   Left on Sumas Way (Hwy 11) to U.S. Customs. Enter the building and check in as a

pedestrian before walking
your bicycle past the booth.

Proceed south through
Sumas on Cherry Street.

6.0 Left on Garfield Street.

6.1 Right on Sumas Street. The
city park is on your right.

6.9 Left on Front Street.

7.2 Right on Hovel Road.

9.2 Straight ahead on North
Telegraph Road where
Morgan Road intersects. You
have glimpses of the Sumas
River as you ride past dairy
farms, eventually gaining
height.

14.2 Right on Sorenson Road.

15.0 Left on Breckenridge Road.
Nooksack Elementary
School is on your left. After
a gradual descent, the road
becomes Madison Street
as it enters Nooksack.

17.4 Cross the railway tracks,
then immediately go right
on Nooksack Road (SR 9).

17.6 Right into Nooksack
City Park. Picnic tables,
toilets.

17.6 Backtrack left on
Nooksack Road.

17.7 Left on Madison Street.

18.2 Left on 4th Street
(Gilles Road).

20.5 After passing Alm Road,
stay straight ahead where
Lindsay Road (unmarked)
branches left.

23.0 Left on North Telegraph
Road, which becomes
Hovel Road.

28.4 Left on Front Street.

28.7 Right on Sumas Street.

29.5 Left on Garfield Street.

29.7 Right on Cherry Street and
proceed through Canadian
Customs.

30.2 Right on 2nd Avenue and
retrace your outward route
via Boundary Road and
Whatcom Road.

35.0 Left on Vye Road after
the railway tracks.

35.2 Right to Upper Sumas
Elementary School.

> 45 LOWER SAMISH VALLEY

Skagit County, U.S.

. . . . .

ROUND TRIP	33.9 km (21 miles)
TERRAIN	Paved roads; mostly flat
TRAFFIC VOLUME	Low
ALLOW	2 ½ to 3 ½ hours
HIGHLIGHTS	Quiet roads among farms, Samish River, Bay View State Park, Padilla Bay, artists' galleries in Edison
PICNIC SPOT	Bay View State Park at 22.7 km
STARTING POINT	Edison School Road, near Edison Café
HOW TO GET THERE	BY CAR: From Chuckanut Drive (SR 11), turn west on Bow Hill Road and drive 1.6 km to the Edison Café at Edison School Road. Or turn off Interstate 5 at exit 236 and proceed west on Bow Hill Road to Edison (about 6 km).
	BY TRANSIT: There is no convenient transit option available at this time.
WHEN TO GO	See varied crops and fields of cultivated flowers in spring.

A S THIS ride begins south of the U.S. border, carry the required identification and medical insurance. This easy, pastoral ride takes you through the heart of a fertile valley to the shores of Padilla Bay. Quiet roads unroll between fields of vegetables, grain, fruit and flowers. From its beginning in the Cascades foothills, the Samish River winds lazily across the plain to slide through estuarine marsh into Samish Bay. Below the bridge on Bay View–Edison Road you'll see tugs and gillnetters moored on the riverbank and ancient wrecks lying stranded in the mud at low tide.

From aptly named Farm-to-Market Road you'll descend to a beach picnic site at Bay View State Park, from where you can look across Padilla Bay to March Point and Fidalgo Island beyond.

Take time to browse through the artists' galleries (open at weekends) in the quaint little town of Edison, or finish with coffee and pie in the friendly Edison Café.

KM THE ROUTE

0.0 Edison Café. East on McTaggart Avenue, which becomes Bow Hill Road.

1.6 Cross Chuckanut Drive (SR 11). Rhododendron Café is on the corner. Continue on Bow Hill Road past the cheese stall on the left.

3.1 Right on Bow Cemetery Road. Some graves date back to the 1860s.

3.7 Right on Worline Road.

6.9 Keep right on Ershig Road. Dairy farms.

7.4 Right on Field Road.

8.0 Cross SR 11. Pass the quarterhorse ranch.

9.5 Left on Thomas Road. Cross the Samish River.

11.1 Cross Allen West Road. Orchards and berry farms.

12.8 Right on Benson Road at the T-junction. Raspberry fields.

15.2 Left on Allen West Road.

16.2 Left on Farm-to-Market Road. Uphill!

18.7 Right on Rector Road.

20.9 Right on Josh Wilson Road.

22.0 Right on Bay View–Edison Road.

22.5 Right at the entrance to Bay View State Park, then first left through the underpass to the beach.

22.7 Beach picnic area. Tables, toilets, etc.

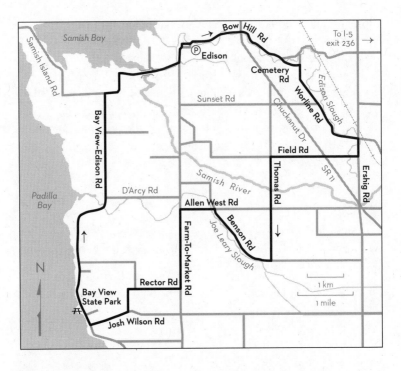

22.9 From the park entrance continue right (north) on Bay View–Edison Road. Gentle hills. Mount Baker is visible to the east.

30.3 Right at the T-junction. Samish Island Road goes left.

32.3 Bridge across the Samish River. View downstream. Old and new boats are moored below the bridge.

33.0 Left on Farm-to-Market Road.

Turn right on McTaggart Avenue in Edison. Quaint buildings and artists' galleries.

33.9 Edison Café.

> INDEX TO RIDES BY DURATION

> ACKNOWLEDGEMENTS

Updating a guidebook would not be possible without the help
of many people and organizations. We wish to thank all those
who contributed their time, knowledge and assistance.

We thank cycling friends for their company and suggestions; in
particular, we are grateful to Barbara Loewi and Tom Hansen for
testing certain of our rides and ably reporting their findings. We
appreciate, too, those unknown cyclists encountered along the way
who were generous with local knowledge and good cheer. The
staff of visitor centres, museums and parks patiently supplied us
with information and material in whatever form we asked for it.
We acknowledge the expertise of editorial staff at Greystone Books
in putting together all the bits and pieces, and we wish to thank
Senior Editor Lucy Kenward for her contributions and guidance
throughout the project.

We hope the finished product reflects these combined efforts
and ensures that *Easy Cycling around Vancouver* remains a
reliable guide.